Published by
Bernard Prince Pu

Copyright © 2016 by Bernard Prince

All rights reserved. No part of this book may be reproduced in any form without written permission from the publisher or writer. All scripture is referenced by the King James Bible.

Dedication Page

This book is dedicated to my parents Deacon Robert Lee Prince and musical song bird Anna Prince.

In addition this book is also dedicated too all that are my family, friends and all that speak these prayers of prophecy. May you be blessed and now began to speak the prophetic prayer under, on and above your life and the earth.

For All The Deep Folk ☺

I apologize if this book of prayer is not deep enough for you. It is intended to be practical, uncomplicated and plainly written. Sometimes we become waxed in the ecclesiastic way of speaking to individuals that possess the ways of the deep mindful mapping systems of the mind, and forget the true heart of prayer which is the way of entering and exiting of Gods' presence. My next book will take us a little deeper but for now I am keeping it light and simple so that prayer can be heard and simplified for all.

This book is first intended for those that do not have a high place in prayer, the beginner, or those that just feel that they want to start a new race. Even if you, the reader is a seasoned warrior I welcome you as well. May God bless us all.

Please, come pray with me…

Foreword from the Author

Dear Champion

    The reason for writing this book is for one reason only. To teach or remind you that your prayers have to be sent out and up in the form of authority, respect and life style. We need to realize that prayer is much more than just asking. Prayer is much more than begging and it is certainly more than complaining. In this book God has allowed me to share what He has given me through my thirty plus years of serious prayer. The prophetic prayer is a spoken prayer of faith that will launch you into a place of battle in the realms of the Spirit and in all other places of authority. In this book you will pray a daily prophetic prayer that will give you a template for your life and style of prayer. I call out into the atmosphere that you find the power in this method of praying and your life be changed by it. This level of praying comes from years of sacrifice and waiting. This book comes from late nights, early mornings and awakened rest from sleep. These pages come from laying on my face, much fasting, joyful and unjoyful experiences, pain and a lot of suffering. In this book you will develop a boldness that you will began to use all day and everyday from this point on. I speak this upon your life NOW in the name of Jesus that you began, this day, to move into the level of the prophetic prayer. I prophetically pray this out into all levels of creation and up-on your life. Get ready, get set, turn the page and let's go…

The Sinner's Prayer

Dear LORD Jesus. I realize that I am a sinner and I am unworthy of your Holiness. I can not stand in your presence because my flesh is a vessel of filthy sin. But I am asking you to come into my life, clean me, up and qualify my person unto righteousness. Reach into my life and change all of my sinful ways into a life of holiness. I am giving you complete authority over my life and my heart is open to you. I believe that you gave your son Jesus to die for the world and that includes me. I believe that you are one God in three persons and I am asking you to come in and save me now. Cover me with the blood of your Son and fill me now with the promise of your Spirit. Now I am yours.
In Jesus name I pray, Amen…
Welcome to the body of Christ.

How To Use This Book

There are 5 ways you can use this book.

1. As a tool for reading only.
2. As a daily prayer for 31 days.
3. As a prayer for 31 days coupled with fasting.
4. As a prayer for 31 days coupled with fasting and the Word of God.
5. As a gift for another.

We do not know where other people are in their prayer life. Some may have never prayed, pray only a little, pray only in a position of need or they could be a womb-ed warrior.

If you are a reader only, that is fine, but please realize that step 4 is the location for the most effective results. If possible pray the daily prayer throughout the day while fasting and read God's Word as the Lord leads you. I guarantee a great result. Whatever level of implementation you choose, 1–5 are all a start in the right direction. In addition, you may decide to choose one level, complete it, then later repeat the process on a higher level to increase your level of intimacy in prayer with our Father.

DAY 1
Today I Prophecy This Pray Up-On My Life

Forgive me oh LORD, of all that I have brought against you. From the deepest parts of my being, I repent of all that has offended you. I come before you now asking for you to cover me in your blood and prepare me for your service by your Word. I believe that Jesus died for my sins and I thank you for all that you have done for me. Accept me into your Holy family and separate me from all sin. I give my life to you now in Jesus name, amen.

Matthew 18:19 powerfully states that *if two of us shall agree on earth as touching any - thing that we shall ask; it shall be done for us by our Father which is in heaven.* Right now, if you are alone, don't worry; I am taking the position of the second person. I am in agreement with you as we pray the Word of God. Right now you must operate in the gift of faith believing that God has given it to you now, out of your mouth say with me out loud, "I RECEIVE THE MANIFESTATATION OF WHAT I NEED NOW THROUGH THE WORD OF GOD."

EXODUS 15:26 *you are the God that healeth me.* So, since you are the God that heals me, I give you the openness that you need to heal me. Submitting all and everything to you, I will not accept any negative reports only the positive Word of God. I receive and pray your Word now. And I also realize that God uses the physician and medication to help in the process if He sees fit.

EPH 3:12 states, *in whom we (I) have boldness and access with confidence by the faith of HIM.* 3:16 - *that He would grant me, according to the riches of HIS glory, to be strengthened with might by His Spirit in the inner man.* 3:19-20 let's me know that *your love passes all knowledge* and *you are able to do exceeding abundantly above all that we ask or think, according to the power that worketh in us.* Deuteronomy 28:2 says that, *all these blessings shall come on me and over take me,* if I shall hearken unto the voice of the LORD thy God. I declare, whatever is of an evil nature, that is in pursuit of me will not over take me. Nothing but the blessings of GOD can over take my being. Then I shall truly be blessed. Any disease that tries to attach itself to me is not of God. God wants all of His children to be blessed in health. Numbers 22:12 fearfully announces the power of God blessing me. And God said unto Balaam, thou shalt not go with them; thou shalt not curse the people: for they are blessed (set apart or un-cursable). I pray to you God with this same statement to those that come to bring any curse upon me, that I am uncursable. Thank you very much Lord. I love you so greatly.

In this time, oh God, I give you my worship. This offering I lay it before you. I need miracle magnification made known to me by eye opening revelation. With unselfish service I sow unto others what I need and desire from you, and from this I receive. It is not about me, but about what God wants of me. And now, this day my demonstration of faith opens up the windows of healing for me and my family. I shall pray until I feel myself rest against you, until you, God invite me in and I will worship in that place. There is a place, God, where you dwell and I'm aggressively consistent in my race. I want the kind of relationship that you want with me. I will pray until I enter in, using praise as my transportation, into a call and response of opportunity with you my Father. *Oh how great is thy goodness, which thou hast laid up for them that fear thee; which thou hast wrought* (formed) *for them that trust in thee before the sons of men.* Psalms 31:19.

Stretch me and fill my capacity until I run over upon others with blessings. I pray in the Spirit, I sing with the Spirit, and I enter-seed in my spirit for the power of heaven to come upon my flesh. In the purest form, I come soaked from the blood of your Son, humbled, asking to come in before you, running in by way of worship. The Holy Ghost takes my worship, transforms it and it bows down before you. I ask that you take these spoken words and make them present before you. I come to the place where I can see you, Father. I ask for your permission to step out of this vessel and come to you. Through you, God, I access all my abilities and move in every gift that I possess.

What am I not doing, that prevents me from taking dominion over my place, and opening and closing what need be. Come, invade my conditions and situations and deliver me. I declare that this is the day of the Lord and not the day my enemy. The chains have been broken but, I need to be set free from this that is trying to stay attached to me. Unlock me now and set me totally free. By your Word I am free and when manifested I am unlooked and in freedom, I dance away from the devices of the enemy.

Ephesians 1:17 – I pray, *that the God of our Lord Jesus Christ, the Father of glory, may give unto you the spirit of wisdom and revelation in the knowledge of him*, so that I may know Him better. Enlighten the eyes of my heart so that I may know the hope of my calling and inheritance. In Ephesians 2:6 it states: *And hath raised us up together, and made us sit together in heavenly places in Christ Jesus.* So, how can sickness or disease defeat me? I know that I am Gods workmanship, created in Christ Jesus to do good works, which God prepared in advance for me to do. For you, oh Lord are my peace. Through Jesus I have access to the Father by the Spirit, allowing me to have great insight into the mysteries of Christ revealed by your Spirit. I take hold of the unsearchable riches of Christ and within this I enjoy my excellent health. In Him and through faith in Him, I may approach God with freedom and confidence. So, because of this, I will not be discouraged because of my sufferings.

Romans 5:1 speaks clearly that, *therefore being justified)* (made right) *by faith, we have peace with God through our Lord Jesus Christ*, through whom I have gained access by faith into this grace in which I now stand. And we rejoice in the glory of God. Not only so, but I also rejoice in my sufferings, because I know that suffering produces perseverance, character, and hope. And hope does not disappoint me, because God has poured out His love into my heart by the Holy Spirit, whom He has given me. I pray that out of His glorious riches that He strengthens me with power through his Spirit in my most inner being, so, that Christ my dwell in my heart through the gift of faith. And I pray that, I being rooted and established in love, that I may have power, together, with all of the saints, grasping how wide and how long and how high and how deep is the love of Christ for me. And to know that this love surpasses all knowledge that I may be filled to the untold fullness of God - Himself. And now to Him which is able to do immeasurable more than all I ask or imagine, according to His power that is at work within me, to Him be the glory in the church and in Christ Jesus throughout all generations, for ever and ever.

In Jesus name, I pray, AMEN...

DAY 2

DAY 2
Today I Prophecy This Pray Up-On My Life

In order to receive what I need from God I live a life worthy of the calling I have received. I shall be humble, gentle, be patient, posturing with one another in love, I will make every effort to keep the unity of the Spirit – just as I was called to one hope, you were called to one hope. When He ascended on high, He led captives in His train and gave gifts to man. To your interruption only I am open. Interpret your tongue to me; bringing me to the place of El Shaddai – (God all mighty). This is where I'll rest until restoration restores my house and joy becomes my garden. I will stay there until my porch is restored, stable, and able to welcome your feet faithfully in the direction of my doors. Now I am unfastened, enter into my place of worship. Inhabit me oh LORD until my windows open freely and you pour out heavily, living waters on my inheritance. Attach your Spirit to my possessions. Be the protector of all my property and health. Allow the curse to pass me by, for my fear is of you. And by this wisdom is your shadow when I stand under the Son.

To wait on you is to lie in the promise of your Word. I will wait on you in the morning. I will wait until you come. In the evening I will remember our pass times and smile. These diseases, pains and visual effects can not disturb me or have dominion over me.

I trust every word out of your mouth and laugh out loud because you are too strong for them. Who can come against me and be successful when I cry out for you to come? I will not look at the negative, only you, the positive. Come closer so I can see you. Come until I smell the scent of heaven. My night shall be days of sunshine and health all the days of my life. Like a flag I wave my blood-stained personhood and declare this body victorious. I take hold of the alter horns and stay there until you release me. Come now, oh great Lord and find me there, fight for me. I need to be free so I can minister freely and be enabled to move free of charge and to take freedom passionately. Be in front of me while I'm undecided and unsure. Speak out loud for me while I'm down, but soon to get up.

I take all that is mine and I place it at your feet. Remembering that it's not mine, but yours and I'm just fine with that. Everything that is good for me comes from you. Allow me to invest in the thing that brings growth and not loss. You have allowed me to possess the possessions of your hand and I dance with them before you and they are locked around my neck. Your Word has sentenced me to life in your kingdom and I gladly serve you there. I am chained by covenant and protected by your grace and mercy-so be it. I shall do the will of the Father and rejoice in every fall and in every step. Your signature is on my forehead. I have been sealed with the ID of the kingdom and not one weapon shall come and over take me. Who can come against me when I call on your great name, **JESUS – JESUS – JESUS**....

    I search for you and the light appears. This light is the light of the whole world and it over takes me. All darkness has to flee from me. All sickness is destroyed and falls at my feet and I dance away. And now I run to your arms my freedom fighter, the one who sets me free. Thank you my Lord and Savior, Christ Jesus, I bow and serve thee. Allow me to lie at your feet for I am humbled. Allow me to embrace you for I am no longer alone. Permit me to love you the way you would have me to love. Comfort me Lord with gladness and safety. In you I am free of all things and I have peace. My feet wade in your joy and I announce our courtship without breach. Unshakeable is my foundation toward actions or any spoken word. No one can convince me of any fabrication that is cast towards you. You are the only truth.

    Lonely am I, Lord without you. Peace I can not find if I can't hear you. I am lost if I can not find you. Please hide yourself not from me. You are my Shepherd and I will never want another. When I hear your voice my soul is restored and my table set. You are my strength when I'm in trouble, and I thank you. My heart is not troubled because I believe in you. Nothing or no one can separate me from you-not tribulation, or suffering, or persecution, or shortage, or nakedness, or danger nor death. Romans 8:37 *Nay, in all these things we are more than conquerors through him that loved us.* In all these things I am more then a conqueror through you because you love me.

Now I am convinced that neither death nor life, nor angels, nor principalities, nor powers, nor the things present, nor the things to come, nor height, nor death, nor any other creature, shall be able to separate me from your love God, which is in Christ Jesus, my Lord. (Romans 8:35, 37-39). No one can say that you are Lord, but by the Holy Ghost. And by the Holy Ghost you have blessed me with gifts and the ability to use them. The manifestation of these gifts that you have given to me is for me, and others like me to profit withal. Thank you for this my God.

Thank you for the Word of wisdom - which enables the praying warrior to move effectively in the spirit with manifested words of wisdom. Thank you for the Word of knowledge that gives me, your warrior, the surety and confidence to move in the whatever, due to the right now information I need to break free. This word enables me to set myself and others free and to continue to stand in the places of success.

Thank you for the gift of faith that I take up like a sword, now, and run passionately towards the gift of healing. I am in agreement with other warriors around the world at this time in prayer. If I'm in need of a gift, which I can't move in at this present time, I connect with intercessors around the world in agreement until it breaks.

I stand in the place where the working of miracles manifests on a Word basis. Please speak into my situation so I may testify of your goodness towards me. Prophecy is in my mouth and I speak the words of my God everyday. I encourage myself before I encourage others. Reveal to me those things that I need to know. I move in the gifting of discerning of the Spirit and you show me who, what, where and how I must move. Thank you. Tongues and the interpretation of tongues is my privileged level and I fight there.

When I suffer the body suffers with me. The love of your children is fashioned by you. When I rejoice, the body rejoices with me and together we fight and win. You are my source. You are my help and my friend. I hold on to you until you answer. I stay before you until you notice me and respond to my gazing behavior. I believe your every word and boast until my enemies hide themselves away from me. I am the righteous and I see you in the Word and you speak to me in this way. No formulas and conjuring of any kind can fool your deliverance for me. And when I call on you things pause because you listen for me. Nothing can stand against you. No-nothing.

I PRAY THIS PRAYER IN THE ALMIGHTY NAME OF YOUR SON, JESUS. AMEN.

DAY 3
Today I Prophecy This Pray Up-On My Life

The standards of life can not hold me back from my place in God. The obstacles that I face encourage me to sow in the Spirit and not into my flesh. I cross the valley of average. My resource and my access comes from the overcoming of the valley experience that I cross over. I refuse to be average or lean to the negative. From these places change will happen. My expectation in you God is over and beyond my valleys. When I am in the valley you are there with me. And as I go through the valley we talk and you make me comfortable. Before I realize it I have made it through what I was going through and I announce that it was all because of you. In the valley it rains but you cover me. If I injure myself there you deal with it in that place. There I rest in you and you give me confidence in my sleep. Thank you. I go to the valley freely because my lesson is there. But in this lesson you are with me guiding me through. As I go through you occupy my mind and I'm alert to your voice and what you show me. When the pain become excessive it ushers me in the Holy Place and my praise comes before you crying out for more of you and less of me. You are a present help in my trouble so I march inside of it. You are inside of my trouble. So come and make known your glory in me in that place. In these times my righteousness will not be hidden for my faith is not sin.

The things that are in the valley define just who and what I am. And I increase in faith and power under the truth of my Lord and Savior. I am balanced within victories and trouble. And now my faith is increased. Some places in the valley are beautiful but difficult to come within reach of. But you give the plan of possession to me and I take it. I may be afraid of what I have to go through, to snatch hold of it, but I hear your voice and I increase in my strength and confidence. To see you is to stand on the cleft and look over. To feel you, I must come where you are. And you are found there, in the valley. Your grace is more than enough for me and in my valley you are full of grace. In this place is terror, embarrassment, discomfort and negative rooted situations but – all of heaven is surrounding me. I matter to you God and you have let down the net of rescue for me. I live within the war zone protected. David said "yea though I walk through the valley of the shadow death I will feel no evil" because you are found to be in the valley with me.

Psalms 23:4 Yea, though I walk through the valley of the shadow of death, I will fear no evil: for thou art with me; thy rod and thy staff they comfort me.

Genesis 26:19
And Isaac's servants digged in the valley, and found there a well of springing water.
In the valley times oh LORD I will dig deep

inside myself. I will dig until I find you my source of life. In the book of John the fourth chapter and the fourteenth verse you tell me that if I drink of the water that you shall give to me I shall never thirst. The water that you shall give me shall be in me a well of the water springing up into everlasting life. I may have valley times but God is with me. The Word is over my life. Prophecies have been spoken over my life. God is consistent in my life. The Word of God has come to my life and I am obedient to server Him. I am secure in God and I am blessed pass any measure and I hold the authority to do what I need to do in Christ Jesus. God made me in His image and I have the look of holiness responding in faith. I am found hiding in God for He is my victory in battle. The influence of heaven is upon me and by the Word the angels come and fight for me until I stand with all evil surrounding me fallen. The judge of heaven and of earth has come against all that try me and He speaks penalties against them on my behalf. Every hindrance and interference has been spoken against by the mouth of the Father who is LORD, the Master of everything.

Lord I need your help. I worship until the heads of the giants are in my hand. I am the stones in David's pouch. I wait until I am released from the sling. I will not lower myself and my standard to live or agree with the enemy. I will fight until the sword of the LORD has thrust itself in the throat of the adversary. With your help I will stand until you have come. With His hand He has come to bring me boldness. The name of the LORD is upon my house and anything that is not like my God is a trust passer and is in contempt of the court of the LORD. Now I rejoice in ownership and position calling on the name of the Lord. God has raised a crop in me and the harvest has come inside of my spirit ready to be a gift unto the LORD. I give tithe on all that He has blessed me with and His alter stands before me. My sacrifice is ready to be present before the LORD. Our worship is untouched for it is the LORDS'. There is no parcel praise inside of me. My faith is in the LORD who brings confidence and assurance.

    I release all that is old and receive the newness of God. My needs are met by the table that has been set in the presence of my enemies. I praise at the mention of your name. I lift you until I come out. I shall worship and magnify you in the new place of blessing and the faithfulness of my God.

    I speak to myself until my flesh bows down into a place of Holy submission. I hear God speaking and I request more of Him. I announce to the earth that I am in the place where I belong and I minister to the people of this earth. I speak to the north, to the south, to the east and to the west to repent and cry out to the Lord until He comes. And when He comes He brings His glory with Him for He is the light of heaven and the beauty there of.

In my mind I imagine us together. God is in my mind, heart, sole and body. I have the appetite and the craving for Gods presence. The power of the Spirit of God is in me and I receive that power for my growth and way of living. I will not be lazy and then crave the things of others. God is the source of all that I need and I commit to the will and the ways of God. These things I declare in the name of my Lord and savior Jesus Christ.

I align my mind, my mouth and my sight in the will of God. The will of God is the target that I aim for in this my sights are set to the center of His will. These things I speak upon my flesh and I believe that the reward has come due to my searching of Him.

My reward is at my hand and the decision of life is around my waist. Easy is the prayer that I call out to Him because God and I talk all the time and at anytime. My offerings honor God. God is excited about my life because of the relationship that we share. I love God and He loves to hear my worship coming towards His throng. When we talk He makes me glad and I return shortly to His presence.

Restore me oh Lord for I am empty. I call on you to fill me to overflow. I need an experience with your fullness and mercy. I say to the sinner God is my supply and my foundation. Lord, show the sinner your glory on me. I will openly shout praise to you.

You have released me and I am no more captive to the world but captive in Christ.

Amen and amen.

DAY 4
Today I Prophecy This Pray Up-On My Life

I am grateful to you oh Lord for all that you have done. I am not in bondage any longer. I am releasing the power of the Word daily in my life and right now I am free. I am a doer of the Word. I am the temple of God down here on earth. I am the righteousness of God and I move in authority to the binding of all that is against me.

I change the way that I think daily according to the Word of God. I will overcome. I will bless the Lord at all times and His praise shall always be in my mouth. The visitation of the Lord is continuous and we remain friends forever. My voice is lifted and my praise surrounds His throng. He laughs in joy because I praise Him so. My song is a jewel on the finger of God. I love to sing to you early in the morning.

I will not lay down my anointing for the things of this world. I will not turn in my crown for the riches of the earth. I will not hand over my holiness to the spirit of whoredom. I shall run until I reach the territory of God. I respond in the motivation of the Word of God and the changing power of the Father that is in heaven. Amen.

I live to the perfection of the Master and the excellence of heaven is in my sight. I lock all my vision and aim to the location of lust and I come against it in anointed confrontation to the tearing down of what is not like Him. I am anointed to live a power packed Word touching structure and standard killing daily what comes to hinder me.

My life is authoritive to the pulling down. My mouth is open to speak unto obedience. My steps are ordered and I follow in the steps of the Lord now and forever. My next level of life and freedom is a level of the fight of victory. I pursue Him for my deliverance and protection. I am sold out to God and there is no sale for the devil for he is not my father. All things are pulled down in the realm of the spirit and I visit this place until I receive my assignment and then comes my victory.

I prophecy to myself encouraging my sole to prosper in Him. I belong to the shifting of the Spirit of God to the empowering of placement. I walk in the divine presence of God. Conceal in me the tests of my life until remembrance and humbling belongs to my flesh. During my assignment I remember what you have done and I continue in my journey. My life is a book to myself and I appreciate where you have brought me from and now I have purpose. You're assignment for me is mine to live in victory and testament.

My stages of faith are walked out daily and

developed until maturity. My decisions are clear and they are in the will of God. I associate my eyes with the things of God. I set my eyes hating the things that God hates. I am careful of what I take in and I guard every gate with trumpets and shouting unto the Lord.

I will speak to the aroused temptations that have come to divide the relationship that I have with my Lord and savior Jesus Christ. In my suffering I am purified in the fire and I come out as pure gold. Value and greatness is hung around my neck. I will be safe in the presence of God and I will speak to temptation, with the Word, like Jesus spoke to satan when He was tempted by him. I come against fear with the Word of God. Proverbs 29:25 The fear of man bringeth a snare: but whoso putteth his trust in the Lord shall be safe.

Right now I come against the possession of evil over me with the Word of God. Proverbs 28:10 Whoso causeth the righteous to go astray in an evil way, he shall fall himself into his own pit: but the upright shall have good things in possession.

With the help of heaven I come against all obsessions that come to overtake me with the Word of God.

Exodus 15:9
The enemy said, I will pursue, I will overtake, I will

divide the spoil; my lust shall be satisfied upon them; I will draw my sword, my hand shall destroy them.

Exodus 15:10
Thou didst blow with thy wind, the sea covered them: they sank as lead in the mighty waters.

Exodus 15:11

Who is like unto thee, O LORD, among the gods? Who is like thee, glorious in holiness, fearful in praises, doing wonders?

In the name of our Father who is in heaven I come against all forms of delusion and I am victorious. Joshua 7:13 Up, sanctify the people, and say, Sanctify yourselves against to morrow: for thus saith the LORD God of Israel, There is an accursed thing in the midst of thee, O Israel: thou canst not stand before thine enemies, until ye take away the accursed thing from among you. Now, at this time, I give God permission to remove the accursed thing that come in the form of delusion in my life at this time. Lord, live in me.

To the spirit of oppression I speak these words to you in the name of Jesus. Psalms 119:134 deliver me from the oppression of man: so will I keep thy precepts. In the name of Jesus I come against the spirit of depression by these words of my deliver.

Galatians 5:17
For the flesh lusteth against the spirit, and the spirit against the flesh: and these are contrary the one to the other: so that ye cannot do the things that ye would.

Isaiah 59:19
So shall they fear the name of the LORD from the west, and his glory from the rising of the sun. When the enemy shall come in like a flood, the Spirit of the LORD shall lift up a standard against him.

Satan has brought an assault on me at my weak positions. My thoughts, my sexual immorality, my greed, behavior that is unholy, dishonesty, unholy conduct, all envy and evil speaking. Any nasty misrepresentation, abusiveness, pride, foolishness, recklessness or thoughtlessness is broken now by me speaking against it with the Word of God.

Mathew 12:34-35
O generation of vipers, how can ye, being evil, speak good things? For out of the abundance of the heart the mouth speaketh. A good man out of the good treasure of the heart bringeth forth good things: and an evil man out of the evil treasure bringeth forth evil things. A bath of unclean waters of unholiness and filthy desires I give to the Lord and now I am free of them.

Mathew 12:35
A good man out of the good treasure of the heart

bringeth forth good things: and an evil man out of the evil treasure bringeth forth evil things. Through faith I am righteous and I am pleasing to God because I live by Faith. Amen…

DAY 5
Today I Prophecy This Pray Up-On My Life

Religious legalism is binding and unfruitful and I stay away from it and guard my faith with the law of God. I may have been blind to what is coming but God is my sight. I know what to say too those that try to confuse me because the Word of God is in my mouth. God is against all that is against me and I rejoice when He comes forth to put in check sinful behavior.

My eyes are open in the spirit realm and I listen to the Holy Ghost that is with-in me. My antenna is up and I am watching. The Sword of the Lord is in my hand and I have been trained to stand and defend my life and my family in prayer. I walk in the Word and I trail in the blood of Jesus. Wherever He walks I place my feet in His steps and I walk in confidence and light. Daily I have peace because I am following Him. My hands applaud and my mouth sings of His will and His ways. With love songs that create passion and thirst I shall drink and pause at His beauty.

I am not bound I am free of all complications. I place my trust in you and I will enjoy my life becuse I trust you. I long for you and I receive your thoughts while I live in ease. I have not lost my peace and all struggle I trust it to you Father. I am not negative and I have no doubt in you because you are the righteous one.

I will not allow satan to steal from my life anymore. The truth is setting me free day by day. I will not allow anything that you hate to control my mind and my heart. I am not bound by the things of the world but I am free and I am the child of the King of glory. Who is the King of glory; you are Lord, strong and mighty in my battles. I live at the feet of Jesus and I listen to you and I rest in you at all times. I am not full of doubt I am free by the Word. I am not chained by fear but free to fear God. The fear of God is to respect Him in everything that I say and do and I am free as well as increased to sever Him. I am a conqueror and I desire to seek His face daily. I will not hide or be found sneaking around in sin because I hate what God hates and I have no desire for sin to rest on the steps of my temple. My temple is Holy and I keep it clean by what I allow to enter and to exit.

My worth and my values are not determined by what is surrounding me. I refuse to be effected by the song of the world and its interpretation. My influence is found in the Word of God. My joy comes to me in the form of a sanctified song. My dance that dances is the vehicle that comes in time of trouble and becomes my rescue. Victory is sweet everyday.

I may not be perfect but He is perfect in me because I follow the leadership of the Master. Whatever it takes I will break free. The portrait of God is in my heart. The law of God is in my heart. The leadership of the Holy Spirit in every way is in me. Meaning, ANY WAY, I will trust in the leading of the Lord. I am not subject to the elementary ways of this world. The Spirit of God is speaking to me and mastering me. I pray to the Father that He becomes the small and the large things in my life. I am in consistent fellowship with God. I live a life of prayer and fasting reaping the joy of my harvest.

    I am anointed to do what I need to do. I will trust in the Lord and believe in the help that comes to me from the throng of heaven. I shall do what He requires of me and my relationship is under the wings of His grace and His mercy. I will wait on you and the foolish yoke shall burst into. This I will not allow to corrupt and complicate my life. I am in the plan of a Holy God and I take His ways to be serious and foundational against all approach. I am free in the fog of my circumstances.

    My joy laughs in the Lord and I believe it. I forgive my enemies and I lift their heads. I look at my ways and I make Holy my decisions and I trust in the Lord. It may not make since in the natural but in the spirit it is made understandable. I am not lead by my thoughts or my emotions. I am lead by the Lord and my faith is ready at all times to trust in the Lord. The joy of the Lord is my strength and I strengthen myself by the joy that I have. I live to forgive and I have learned to detach from the things that steal my joy. I will live in the simplicity and the ease of the King.

Who is the King of glory? The God that I serve is that King.

I will not choose my love ones over God. I will attend to the things of God and I shall be renewed everyday. I my not understand what you have in front of me but I'll trust you in those right now moments. Lord, I choose you over the things offered to me. My deliverance is in my choosing. I would rather be in you then suffer in my selfishly ways. My sins have been forgotten and thrown in the sea of forgetfulness. My walk with you is my choice and I am now, at this time, walking in agreement with you. Blessed is your most Holy name.

Lord you are bringing the things out of me that have been found dormant inside me. I except your Word and receive the results of the Word. The dormant things that are in me are now collecting against my flesh pushing and pulling against my sole and purposed until I bow in acceptance. I am motivated by the function that is divine in me operating and moving until the inside breaks on the outside.

This pressing is for my development in you and I do except it. You are working in me to the perfection of my understanding. Intimacy is in this development and I feel your power changing me folding and folding me. I go through these things and I pass by the holiness that shields me in the surrounding of your attendance that forms me into your pattern. Tie me down to your purpose. My life hinges on the work of God.

Your hedge holds my sacrifice. Because of my situation you have made it possible for me to present to you a sacrifice. Bondage is released through the sacrifice. I have and will continue to break free because you have allowed my sacrifice to be caught in bush-like places and I thank you. I live in freedom through the sacrifice. I am caught in the bush of opportunity. I am caught in the purpose of God. I have been positioned by the needs of interceding for someone else. I have been caught up to serve. I surrender to the purpose of the sacrifice.

I walk one step and I bow to you in worship. I pick up my ministry and take one step and I fall at your feet. I pick up the temple and I take one step and I fall at the sound of your voice and I cover my flesh because I am filthy before you. I wave the blood stain banner and all that is surrounding me collapses and I shout and play my instrument while in your presence. My life moves hazard free due to the caution of my steps for your Holiness requires constant acknowledgment of what I am holding. You have over taken my desire to be thoughtful and obedient to my assignment. You are too holy for me to dishonor the lifting of your divine nature. Because of my fear of you, you have changed my name in heavenly places.

Praise be to your name…

DAY 6
Today I Prophecy This Pray Up-On My Life

Whatever the enemy unleashes against me will not be able to lock its bite of attack on me. The direction that I travel is the direction of the LORD. By the authority of my mouth I speak to it and it discontinues its forwardness and direction leaving me unharmed. Its strategies are defeated and routed away from me. The attack against my body has failed. The attack against my finances has been unsuccessful. The attack against my marriage has wasted away. Because of this that the Lord has done I am able to resist and encouraged to run towards the life that GOD has set in His plan for me.

I prophesy that I am in the reaping season of my life and I will not faint. My faith is growing and I refuse to be frustrated and oppressed. My hope is strong in the LORD. I set myself free by the freedom of the Word and I boldly come before you LORD in submission and joy. You are my liberty. You are the owner of my soul and not a guest. My contractual agreement by covenant I show to all that come to take possession of me and my abilities.

As I sing to you I am set free and you give me new freedom everyday. When I awake hell knows that the warrior of GOD has awakened. When I suffer I suffer in the Lord and I am coming out when my faith is built up in the Lord. I am greater then all that is not in the LORD. My faith is not in things but it is in my God. My faith is my power and things can not give me faith. My faith is a song of travailing and the working of patience. I will wait on the progress of the LORD. I walk in faith. I am delivered by my faith. I am a product of my faith.

My place is a place that has to be finished so I may know the enemy in that place. Though it may be disguised I still know it and my response is to defeat it again. I will continue to pray until I hear from my Father and I am satisfied.

If I don't hear from GOD in my time I am confident that my will is not done but GODS will is. GOD allows the strength of my inner man to be the strength that is the same strength of heaven. I am transformed through not giving up on GOD. My faith knows that if GOD doesn't do what I ask He is still GOD. GOD is still my GOD in my misunderstanding of His moving. The face of satan is frowning due to my faith in my Father. The altering of my life is solely done by my Father. The devil has no control over me for I trust in my Father which art in heavenly places.

I am no longer living in the place of darkness. I am now an heir unto salvation. I do not face the powers and principalities of wickedness in my own strength. He has given me power and authority over all of the powers of the enemy. Through the blood and the Word of GOD I am able to pull victory down to myself and live in success.

GOD allows the hidden things to be revealed to me. We are the over comers of this world. I am the child of GOD that seeks out the battle field to war against the enemy. My inner most being is in the way of the LORD. The springs of life flow from my heart and my heart longs for you. I receive GOD in my thoughts and I believe His promises. In this place I receive the thoughts and the Word of faith. This is the place where my will, desires, emotions and all other mental abilities are located and I give GOD reign over all of them.

For in my inner being I delight in GOD'S law; but I see another law at work in the members of my body, waging war against the law of my mind and making me a prisoner of the law of sin at work within my members **Romans 7:22-23.**

I take aggressive actions against the devil and his works bringing all thoughts that are not like GOD into captivity by the Word. I renew my mind everyday while I receive new mercies and grace from my Father that is in heaven. While filling my heart and mind with the Word of GOD I can withstand all that comes against me and I live in total success everyday. Amen.

GOD has not given me the spirit of fear, but of power, love and a sound mind. GOD has made me to be mobile in my life and in the spirit. Satan is a liar and he will not overtake me. He has no control over my mind, my thoughts, emotions and everything that I possess, that is good. All that is victory comes from GOD.

I love GOD and I live in His love and kindness. He is my strength and my power. The only picture that I think to paint of GOD is a picture of love.

Today, I declare, that satan is a liar. I will not be subject under his power today. I will not give satan power over my person and by the Word satan, you are defeated. I resist your works and I rejoice in the name of Jesus. I am full of truth. I am full of peace. I am full of joy. I am full of the Word of GOD.

The Word Is MY

Aggressive Action

___

Violent Weapon in Battle

___

Full Armor

___

Garment of Glory
_____

Trumpet of Sound
_____

Path of Righteousness
_____

Voice of Authority
_____

Covering in Open Times
_____

Choice of Truth
_____

Counter Attacks Against The Enemy
_____

Victory
_____

Humble Heritage
_____

Identifying Mark
_____

Flag of Uniqueness

_____

Display of My Character

_____

Blood Covering

_____

Template

_____

To God Be All Glory, Amen…

DAY 7
Today I Prophecy This Pray Up-On My Life

I win the battle of my mind. I overcome the strategies of all that come and desire me. Whatever comes to lure me into the cycle of death will never manage to discontinue my works in the Lord. Though they study me they will never conclude my destiny. My conclusion is deep inside of the Lord. I am free to power up in the Spirit of God. The power of God has been promised to me and my descendents. I face all things in the power of heaven. By this power I counterattack the stance of the enemy in the battlefield of my mind. Every stronghold that has operated in my life, at this time, has been defused by the promises of God in His Word.

I am set free from the approach of the enemy. My life has been in a special editing process in the studio of the Master. My training manual is the bible. Instead of breaking down I break free. I break through as the Spirit reminds me of what, and how, God has delivered me from. Through this I learn to live everyday life. God I need you on a daily basis. Present your plan for me and I will study it until you are satisfied with me.

By your mouth I've become skilled. By your hand I am delivered all the day long. In your bosom my head rest and in your heart I am found. You come to me while I am asleep and I feel you smile. I awake in the song of the LORD and I sing back to you what you've sung to me while I rest in my sleep. My instrument is finely tuned and ready. My strings are to harp.

The curtain is pulled back and I come into you holy. This dance that I ballet is with you and no one else. My feet are above the earth and I take wings towards you with every beat of my heart. This is a place for you and I come now close my LORD. My flesh is nowhere to be found closed to you. This place is like sleep unto rest, seed to soil and lighting reviving deep into my earth. You are the balance to my every need and I need to love you LORD. You keep me balanced.

The LORD has given me insight on the place of my battle and I prepare my spirit for war. GOD is giving me a line of attack and I assemble in opposition to wait until GOD sends heaven with my word and my help. Now I am prepared and equipped to defeat satan and his host. Now in the meantime I set worship at my boarders and the fire of heaven protects me and my sight is made clear. I am now the one in pursuit of the enemy and I will over take and concur all.

I will stay with GOD until I see my victory and then I will stay even longer. My halleluiah is bold and loud and I aim it towards my GOD and my enemy. I am living in the overflow of blessings now and I fall at His presence. I will come to the house of GOD and tell my story and He will reply "I know. Its okay now I'm here." I am in the place where I can hear Jesus and I call out to Him with a cry of mercy. I will not stop until you come to me. I will not leave or hang my head because I am not listening to man I listen for you.

I am moved only by the Word of GOD. This problem does not change my stance with my Father that is in heaven. My prospective is on the power of His presence. The counterattack of the enemy misses me by great distance and the hand of GOD lands on his jaw. The dominion of power is greater than I have ever known and I sing to Him within it. Everyday is a life changing event and I long to change for the better in Him. I receive new revelation daily in my spirit with such power that it enables me to conquer my flesh levels and resist the attacks with unshakable balance.

I praise you because I know you. I follow you because I hear your voice. The devil will not intimate me and I will not be terrified of Him. In the night GOD is still holy and His light guides me to my place of rest in Him. With GOD nothing is impossible and I ask for the impossible and I receive my request from Him. My faith shall travel straight to the throne of GOD. All things are possible through Christ my savior and Lord. I believe in you Lord. The gifts are functioning deep down within me. Deep in my temple I worship you and your gifts began to flow over into my situations.

Your Word has come to me and you are speaking to my spirit. Suffocate every attack of the enemy and behold, the glory of the LORD is here and all is possible. I have surrendered to you and I am dead to sin. Self covers my flesh but they both are crucified daily for you see them both. I assemble every gate to be obedient to you and your Word. I walk and I pray. I work while I'm on my job and I pray. Late in the evening I sing melodies in my heart to you and you receive them. I lay and sleep while my spirit man takes over in prayer, praise and worship.

My eyes are set on you LORD and I anoint my eyes and you change my vision. I go beyond the torn veil and I call out for you. Then you close the chamber doors and we spend time together. I hunger after and thirst for righteousness. Please come without measure upon my person. I need you to split the seas in my life and call me to come through. I call on you and I am ready to pay the price to hold your hand. I pursue you pantingly. I chase after you. I go after you with passion and trust. I love to spend time with you.

Right now I enter into a place of freedom for my family and I call them by their name and you hear me. LORD GOD my Father stands up now and He looks over my place with authority and pronounces a Word over my life and the life of my family. Speak over my waiting and assemble the angels to come and move on my time in life. Oh LORD I am blessed to move in the authority of 2nd Kings the sixth chapter. My prayer is that you respect my voice and my demand against my enemies. Place this chapter upon all that comes against me in Jesus name, thank you.

You are Holy and I love and adore you for you are the worthy lamb of GOD. You are faithful and you are the lamb of GOD. You are precious and you are the lamb of GOD. You are worthy and you are the lamb of GOD. I weep until you come. You manage my person and my emotions. My hands wait to hold you. My eyes long to behold you. My feet are set to dance before you. I will rejoice inside my test with strength and might while my tears prove to be sincere. Come to me tangible. I open up my doors and you hold back nothing from me. I am spending my time with you and my environment has become a surrounded place of opportunity. I have found life in you and I repent. Daily I am renewed. Take your place in me and set there for ever. You are my full potential and my resource and I rejoice in you. You are my relief and I choose to be identified with you. You are my place to be and I live there with all rest, at your feet. You are my point of contact and nothing is between you and me. I will not settle for anything under your will.

All sickness passes me by. It can not grab hold and take me. By the power of the Holy Ghost all things fall in defeat and the spirit of expectation will not abort itself. There is a desire in me to want more of your feast and your waters. When I fall I call out for you to come. I desire you. I desire to have more of you and I'm expecting the fig tree to give. My desire pushes me closer to you and I cross the dangerous path and you shadow me unseen in the face of the devourer. My place of consecration will not be moved and I run into my break though.

It will not over take me. I have in my possession fruit and not just the leaf. My hunger is not based on famine because you are my provider. How can I be without in you? My miracle is saddled and my feet are made ready to leap and run. The stage is not only set but it is sold out and I will not settle for less. I will have my fruit and the safety to eat it where you direct me.

I will be warned and I will not be deceived. You will respond to the face of my adversary. GOD you are too big for me to worry. I will not worry unto sin. I will deal with the thing that comes against me. I may be under attack due to my mission and ministry but my assignment has come to me from the mouth of my GOD and you know all things. You will not settle for things underneath your will. I am expecting my desire to inflame in me until the things that are not like you are set on fire in me.

You are cursed devil and I shut down your works

that are aimed at me and the body of Christ. I open my mouth and I terminate the words of the enemy. The people that are in my life that means me no good you have set them up against me. You will not pull me down. Lord shut down the war of the people that come to curse me. I break what my father and my mother could not or did not break here on earth and in the spirit realm.

I shall have vision in the ditch. I will survive in the valley of the strange place. I will continue in the vision when no one understands my journey. I will take my vision to the places that challenge me. When I slip my vision shall stay the course of my life. My vision for me is my passion unto my deliverance. It may look like defeat to others but to me I see victory through my God given vision. My vision causes me to hear what others can not hear nor understand. My vision causes me to feel my way through the places of night and fear.

In Jesus name, AMEN...

DAY 8
Today I Prophecy This Pray Up-On My Life

My wealth is confident and my assurance is in you. My worth in Jesus is security and strength is resting upon me now. My finances are lining up with the Word right now as I speak announcing obedience and trust to attach itself on me. My money belongs to GOD. My riches are in the chest of the Master. I am wealthy according to your will for the sake of ministry.

The foreign things I do not understand. But if my GOD tells me to go there he will give to me the translation of the words that are being spoken to my path. I will trust in the LORD within the places of those that are unfamiliar to me. My trust is in the LORD. I will take GOD at His word.

LORD, allow my life to be a life of conduction. My life is a life of fruit and proof of daily gain and not wastes. I am the proof of faith and things line up in truth due to my lifestyle. I am an honest person and I have the proof of my faith. I care not to sin within my relationship with GOD. GOD is not my temp-service. His love is forever and everlasting due to His position in the atmosphere. He is all around. He is over and above preparing my faith to be full.

I look for the manifestation in my life to overtake me and under-gird my faith. My sowing must continue its upheaval and my sowing causes me to be the recipient of the harvest. We are predestined and predetermined to win. I receive from my Father the blessing. He has placed His hand on my head and I have received the announcement of my life freely and in truth. My life is worth living and I hear the voice of the LORD. Something is about to happen in my life. I am here but soon I will be there where the LORD is waving me in. I have received the strength to wait on the LORD. I have cried out for the strength of my place in GOD.

I am living in the great blessing and I see it in the distance. I see the state of my being coming. In the dark place I still grow. It's not what it looks like. My blessing is found waiting in the image of my GOD. I can see the new dimension and they are coming from the Spirit and I spend time there to learn of them. I will now take my new step in the anointing as it advances me forward. I declare whatever it takes. I call it and I stand to receive it now. My issue has been refined and in this process I have been renewed. I will go pass my earthly name and call upon the name of the LORD to change my name.

I Am Blessed Because:

I AM HEALED

I Am Blessed Because

___

I AM RENEWED

___

I Am Blessed Because

___

I AM IN THE WILL OF GOD

___

I Am Blessed Because

___

I AM IN CHRIST

___

I Am Blessed Because

___

I AM IN MY RIGHT MIND

___

I Am Blessed Because

___

I AM FILLED WITH THE SPIRIT OF GOD

___

I Am Blessed Because

_____

GOD IS MY SOURCE

_____

I Am Blessed Because

_____

I AM ATTACHED TO THE FATHER

_____

I Am Blessed Because

_____

GOD IS WORKING IN ME

_____

I Am Blessed Because

_____

I FEAR GOD

_____

I Am Blessed Because

_____

I AM A PRESON OF WORSHIP

_____

I Am Blessed Because

_____

I AM A PERSON OF PRAISE

_____

I Am Blessed Because

_____

I AM A PERSON OF PRAYER

_____

I Am Blessed Because

_____

I MOVE IN THE ATHOURITY OF THE WORD

_____

I Am Blessed Because

_____

MY CHOICES ARE IN THE LORD

_____

I Am Blessed Because

_____

I SPEAK WHAT THE FATHER HAS ALREADY SPOKEN

_____

I Am Blessed Because

_____

I AM COVERED IN THE BLOOD OF CHRIST

_____

I Am Blessed Because

_____

HE IS GREATER IN ME THEN HE THAT IS IN THE WORLD

_____

I Am Blessed Because

_____

I HAVE THE FAVOR OF GOD

_____

I Am Blessed Because

_____

I TRUST IN THE LORD

_____

I Am Blessed Because

_____

MY FAITH IS IN THE LORD

_____

I Am Blessed Because

_____

MY MIND IS ON CHRIST JESUS

_____

I Am Blessed Because

_____

I MOVE BY THE SPIRIT OF GOD

_____

I Am Blessed Because

_____

I GO IN THE MOST HOLY PLACES OF GOD

_____

I Am Blessed Because

_____

GOD IS MY FRIEND

_____

I Am Not Defeated Because

_____

I AM AN OVERCOMER WHILE I'M IN THE TEST

_____

I Am Not Defeated Because

___

I WILL REJOICE IN HIM WHILE I'M IN THE TEST

___

I Am Not Defeated Because

___

I WILL PROCLAIM THE NAME OF THE LORD WHILE I'M IN THE TEST

___

I Am Not Defeated Because

___

THE LORD GOD IS MY TRUTH WHILE I'M IN THE TEST

___

I Am Not Defeated Because

___

I AM CLOTHED IN THE SPIRIT OF GOD WHILE I'M IN THE TEST

___

I Am Not Defeated Because

___

MY WEAPONS, THAT I USE ARE OF THE LORD WHILE I'M IN THE TEST

I Am Not Defeated Because

I POSSESS THE ANOINTING WHILE I'M IN THE TEST

I Am Not Defeated Because

I WALK BY FAITH AND NOT BY THE SIGHT OF MAN WHILE I'M IN THE TEST

I Am Not Defeated Because

I WEAR THE ARMOUR OF THE LORD WHILE I'M IN THE TEST

I Am Not Defeated Because

I PRAY WITHOUT CEASING WHILE I'M IN THE TEST

I Am Not Defeated Because

_____

MY MOUTH IS KEPT POSITIVE WHILE I'M IN THE TEST

_____

I Am Not Defeated Because

_____

DAILY I DENOUNCE EVERYTHING THAT IS NOT LIKE GOD WHILE I'M IN THE TEST

_____

I Am Not Defeated Because

_____

I PRAY FOR THOSE THAT COME AGAINST ME WHILE I'M IN THE TEST

_____

I Am Not Defeated Because

_____

I ENJOY MYSELF IN THE LORD WHILE I'M IN THE TEST

_____

I Am Not Defeated Because

_____

I KNOW WHO I AM IN CHRIST WHILE I'M IN THE TEST

I Am Not Defeated!
I Am Not Defeated!!
I Am Not Defeated!!!

In Jesus the Christ, AMEN…

DAY 9
Today I Prophecy This Pray Up-On My Life

I am set out to destroy the works of the devil through Christ Jesus my strength. And I give my service to the works of the LORD. I believe in the power of faith and what it brings into my hand. My cup is filled with the waters of life and I drink until I am full.

I am in great health. My mind is clear and sanctified. My shoulders are light and my arms are lifted up high to GOD. My hands are free from the chains of captivity and I hold in them the goodness and mercies of my GOD. In His courts I am found worthy through the blood. I call on the courts of heaven to announce me free throughout the entire earth.

GOD, I am out to get your attention. I shall call on you until you come to me. I declare that I have favor with you and this favor allows me to come into the places of mystery in you. When I worship you come to me. When I praise you, you come and dance with me.

When I am bound by things I shall use the chains that have me bound as instruments of praise. I will lift up my chains to you and shake them in your presence until you take them from me or give me the strength that I need to go on with them. With my life I will praise you.

I am not glued to the floor. I shall move when I need to. I see through my ceilings and I sing to you on my cross. I will dance the shackles off of my feet. I will give my last cake to the poor. I will grow in the Spirit of giving.

I will take a daily evaluation of my flesh and remaining parts of my personhood. I will deal with myself and not spiritualize what is in my mind or what is in my spirit. I have been transformed by the renewing of my mind. I renew myself daily.

I come against the spirit of the imposter. I will not give hand to the evil doer. My life is purified by the lamb. Not my will be done LORD. It's your will and not mine. Give me the revival of death and separate me from the worldly lust that has condemned this world. I am under the submission of God and I hear clearly form you. My mind is the thought of God and I meditate on Him and that keeps me free. Transform me God until I am not controlled by my flesh. I will not be under the anointing of another. I am in my move of God. God has a life for me and I am like David in the field when the prophet came to anointing him. What God has given me I shall birth it out and become a sight of holiness and sanctification. I am not looking for the applause of man. I long for the approval of the Father. I have met the author and I am true to Him through the blood of Jesus. I am what God has called me to be. I am not concerned with the, amen of man but of God.

I am dead to sin. I am deaf to wrong doing. I shall get up with the process of God. I will not shake hands with the lust of the world. I will call on the atmosphere of God. I will wash in the blood of Jesus. I will have the life style of holiness and move in the power of God. I can hear the behavior of, behold. I can hear the, BUT GOD in my life. I dream of the casting out of the devil and awake in the shout of my God.

I am strong in the authority of God. The enemy shall not wear me out unto weakness and collapse. My mouth is under authority. My mind is under authority. My entire flesh is under the authority of the holy transformation of God. I have authority over the earth and I call the miracles to come in the possession of my hand. I prophecy that miracles are in my possession now. I speak the miracles into the realm of my name. I can see the power of heaven come to me now and I am a miracle performing in His sight, NOW. Health has come to me and I take it. I enjoy the doors of opportunity in the Spirit and I go through with the shout of my spirit.

The Lord has invaded my being and He is preparing me now for Himself. I will come up to where the Lord is for He is Holy. I will cry out the cry that reaches God. The Lord has the sending ability of my positions and I go in the Lord. Today I will worship and not worry. I shall dress myself in the garments of the Lord and I will sing the chorus of amen. I will sing until I can dance freely and my voice shall reach heaven. I will shout forth until my worship surrounds heaven.

I am not overwhelmed and my outcome is not spoiled. The pages of my life have not been torn form the assignment of God. Gods' presence in my life is extraordinary and plentiful in production. Until God comes and rescues me I will stay here until I hear Him calling me. His virtue comes and it belongs to me and I take it. God is applying his healing balm on my being now as I pray and I ask in faith until I receive. I use the Word of God to train my flesh and I am in control of my flesh. The Lord comes against the tactics of the enemy and I remember the works of God in my life. God is doing the unthinkable in my life and I am within the Great I am.

The Holy Spirit illuminates my being and I am seen in the light of God. God is speaking from my destiny and the Word is ascending and descending on my behalf. Enlighten me oh Lord for I am looking to you. Maximize your strength in me. Create distance between those things that are not clean in your sight.

This is a song that I sing to you:

> High praise is what you shall receive from me
> Yahweh high praise
> Everyday when I awake I smile because it's your today Ya-   way
> Yahweh, Elolm, El Shadi not my way
> My way is your way
> Upon my today

Praise the name of my LORD, Yahweh, and AMEN…

DAY 10
Today I Prophecy This Pray Up-On My Life

I pray for the influence of heaven to come upon me in order for my life to affect the lives of others. Allow my life choices to minister too those that are watching my life. I will be consistent in my walk with you Lord and always call on you for help in time of need. You have the right to bridle my emotions and my response is looking towards you for a sanctified reaction.

I am a minister of the Lord twenty four hours a day. I uphold the statement of faith. My expectations are in you and unreal promises will not tough my flesh to make it speak out of place with you.

With the power of heaven I come against the source of conflict that rises up against my relationship with you. I come against the actions of stubbornness that can hinder my move in God. Selfishness will no longer be a flaw in my life anymore. All things that try to attach it's self on to me will fall at the song of the Father.

God will not hesitate to bless me due to my inconsistencies because I am obedient and loyal to His service. I will stand in the face of my accusers. The harassment of evil announces my affectedness upon the gates of hell.

I will give and I will always have. I will do and I will always receive. I will use more faith and I will have more in the moving of God. I will plant more seed and I will have more harvest. I will believe more in God and the more I believe the more good things will happen for me. I pray for the growth of my faith because my harvest is depending on the level of my faith.

I will bring my issues before the council of the Lord and He will deal with them on my behalf. I will leave the place of the Lord with His agenda in my heart. The Lord of my council has found me in the place of test. And God will always be fair with me.

God has risen up a purpose in my city and I am in the center of authority and I pray there. God shall be the developer of my community and the people of this city will bow down in respect of Him. I will shout in the court of this city from my spirit until I see the Lord. The earth is the Lords and the fullness there of. The authority is in the Word of God upon the lips of His ministers. I will trust in the Lord with my whole heart not wavering to my own ways. I trust in the Lord and in His assignment for the warriors within the city.

I call for the anointing to become superglue substance upon me. I speak the things of God to come and fasten themselves on me for the betterment of myself and of others.

I now collect myself and I come against my adversary. I will stay focused and righteousness points towards my life. I shall choose the weapons of the Spirit and not of my flesh. My person will be present in the form of the Father. By the blood I am covered and I stay there. My point of satisfaction is in the face of the Lord. In these times I will stay before the Lord. He has placed a ring on my finger. My foundation is strong and my total being is safe.

The formula of fear shall not rule over me. The unveiling of the evil one will happen in the timing of God for my victory. An unbridled speech shall not be apart of my life. The over throughing of the power of evil is found within my song. Unlived promises are not found in me. I am a child of God. Lord, inspect me daily until I agree with your will for me inside of this day.

The principles of faith are operating in my life and I am in the understanding of God. God has given me the ability to handle His gifts and His power. God is eternal and I am with Him and His eternalness. The promises of God are in my belly. They are the waters of life in my sole. I turn inside and I speak to Him and I drink from my victories that are won through the within-ness of the Spirit. I praise my God today and I lift my hands in total praise. Thank you for this day of victory that is found in you Father.

AMEN…

DAY 11
Today I Prophecy This Pray Up-On My Life

God is operating inside me and the unlocking of _____ is happening now in my life. I am being unlocked now from all that I speak at this time;

I Am Being Unlocked Now From:

Bad Habits

_____

I am being unlocked now from:

_____

Things that I have no explanation for

_____

I am being unlocked now from:

_____

The failure to trust God

_____

I am being unlocked now from:

_____

Trouble

_____

I am being unlocked now from:
_____

The turning away from what God hates
_____

I am being unlocked now from:
_____

Turmoil
_____

I am being unlocked now from:
_____

Disrespecting my temple
_____

I am being unlocked now from:
_____

The things that I think are too hard for me to handle
_____

I am being unlocked now from:
_____

The selling out of my person (on all levels)
_____

I am being unlocked now from:

All weakness and I put on the strength of Gods kingdom

I am being unlocked now from:

The spirit of settling for ungodliness

I am being unlocked now from:

Little effort towards excellence

I am being unlocked now from:

Poverty in my life and my families lives

I am being unlocked now from:

All negativity

I am being unlocked now from:
_____

The lack of a positive mouth
_____

I am being unlocked now from:
_____

Lack
_____

I am being unlocked now from:
_____

The lack of victory
_____

I am being unlocked now from:
_____

The ability to love and to pray for my enemies
_____

I am being unlocked now from:
_____

Not allowing my love to cast out fear
_____

I am being unlocked now from:
___

Unfaithfulness
___

I am being unlocked now from:
___

The lack of agreement
___

I am being unlocked now from:
___

The lack of desire to bless others
___

I am being unlocked now from:
___

Lack of patience
___

I am being unlocked now from:
___

Lack of compassion
___

I am being unlocked now from:
_____

Lack of increase
_____

I am being unlocked now from:
_____

Bondage spiritually and physically
_____

I am being unlocked now from:
_____

A life of no success
_____

I am being unlocked now from:
_____

The misuse of my life
_____

I am being unlocked now from:
_____

Not standing and facing life's realities
_____

I am being unlocked now from:
_____

Not taking possession over the things that God has put before me
_____

I am being unlocked now from:
_____

Not being specific with God in my prayers
_____

I am being unlocked now from:
_____

Not prophesying and speaking the Word of God over my family
_____

I am being unlocked now from:
_____

Not being thankful
_____

I am being unlocked now from:
_____

Not praying for the world

I am being unlocked now from:

_____

Slothfulness

_____

I am being unlocked now from:

_____

Untimely occurrences

_____

I am being unlocked now from:

_____

Believing that I can't reach for the higher things of this world

_____

I am being unlocked now from:

_____

Generational bondage

_____

I am being unlocked now from:

_____

Unproductive yokes

_____

I am being unlocked now from:
_____

From the want not to change or being changed
_____

I am being unlocked now from:
_____

From the lack of motivation
_____

I am being unlocked now from:
_____

From not finishing my tasks
_____

I am being unlocked now from:
_____

The hindrances of my mind not to overcome whatever
_____

I am being unlocked now from:
_____

Not having the ability to conquer daily
_____

John 8:36 If the Son therefore shall make you free, ye shall be free indeed. I am in agreement with Pastor Bernard Prince, that right now, I am free from all things that come to bind me today.

In the mighty name of Jesus Christ our Lord, AMEN…

DAY 12
Today I Prophecy This Pray Up-On My Life

The Word of God is a penetrating tool that is piercing my personhood now. The Word is washing me unto holiness and sanctification. I will lie at the pool of God and I will wash daily. I am in the experience of God and I will begin anew. I lie before Him and talk with Him and I hold not one victim mentality. I release all bitterness so God can renew me. I will live in the restoring of God and listen to the teaching that comes to His heart.

My tears are healing me and I am free because of my release. At this time now I let go all unto my Father God. Life maybe unfair but my Father is. I focus on the things that God has been for me and not the negative things that are in my life. God I am grateful of what I have. I accept your beauty for my ashes now in Jesus name, amen.

Today is a day of healing for me. The light of Christ comes to me and I embrace it. I am able to do what I need to do today to be accessible to His will. I refuse to be down today. I refuse to be defeated today. I come against all things that come against me today with the Word of God. I receive all that is for me today that is from God.

I am establishing a valuable relationship with

God from day to day and I'm glad in Him. God come down in my heart. I am not full of anger but joy. The cycle of defeat is now broken off of my life and I rise again and again and again.

I have found new accuracies in the vision of the Lord. The sight of God is what I use to set my standards. My earthly sight is enhanced by the bifocal of the Spirit and I see wisely. I do not see with the natural eye but by the sight of God the Father.

The principles of God are my first fruit blessings. My blessings are in the walk of faith and not in my fleshly emotions.

I have the revelation that comes from the mouth of the Holy one. This revelation makes me able to motivate myself to come closer to Him. God is real this morning and I take in the increase of the revelation from the throng.

I give myself to the system of God and I have the revelation to move in the wise places of God and I am refreshed in the Word of God.

I present my life to God every morning and I set my person before Him for approval. I come before you my Lord and my Savior in respect and humbleness. Today I receive the love of the Father.

These things will not overtake me today:

Poverty
___

Will not overtake me today
___

Famine
___

Will not overtake me today
___

Deceases
___

Will not overtake me today
___

Lack
___

Will not overtake me today
___

Confusion
___

Will not overtake me today

The shortage of planning

Will not overtake me today

Evil

Will not overtake me today

No weapon

Will not overtake me today

Manipulations

Will not overtake me today

Thoughts of lust

Will not overtake me today

Wickedness
_____

Will not overtake me today
_____

Laziness
_____

Will not overtake me today
_____

Slothfulness
_____

Will not overtake me today
_____

Ineffectiveness
_____

Will not overtake me today
_____

Being unfocused
_____

Will not overtake me today
_____

This I declare inside my today, in the name of Jesus, Amen.

DAY 13
Today I Prophecy This Pray Up-On My Life

Today God is my source and my supply. The abundance of the Lord is mine. I am diligent in my willingness and my commitment to God is firm and unmovable. My life is full of responsibility unto God and I am faithful to Him. God has invaded me and brought all that is good with Him unto me. My hand is diligent and I am rich. I come into the source of God with joy and gladness.

My life is a life of harvest and I work this field early in the morning. This is my life and I will live it until the Housekeeper calls me to come home. Prosperity is upon me and the yoke of it is easy. When evil calls for me I point to my Lord and Savior and He handles what I direct towards Him.

My supply is in the Lord and I believe in Him. I seek Him and He rewards me in the seen and the unseen. I can not qualify if I can not come into His presence. The Spirit of the Lord up wells from deep down within me and it is water to my sole.

The enemies hand is taken off of my supply and I cry out to the Lord and my God delivers me. The righteousness that is within me transports the belongings of the Father to me. My supply is robed around me. He girds up my lowing and ties up all that is mine and presents it to me for my development in Him.

There is no limit in my place in God and my supply is including towards Him. God has opened doors for me and I move through them with favor and love. My way has been established into the not as though they were and every time I shout things begin to form and I decree them to be so.

The impossible is possible in God and all of my victories are in God. I see accomplishment that has been made preset by my Father. It may not look like I'm moving but I am. It may not look like my ministry is effective but it is effecting boundaries in the Spirit and earth. I will lay down my life and pick up righteousness every time my mind detours from the thinking of God.

God said that I can have it and I want all that He has for me. I elevate myself to praise Him. I speak to myself to worship Him. I believe what God is and has said unto me. I shall speak prophetically and I shall teach prophetically. The prophetical call of the Lord is mine and I live by the predictive revelation of God the Father. God is the light in my mind and I think clearly and freedom is in my mind. My offering and tithe is my style of life and I honor God with my life of giving. My mind is fixed on honoring God to the point of obedience. By this method of living I stay free. I am leaning against the glory of God, being affected by His captivity against me. I want not to be free from Him. I have turned towards Him my captivity surrendering all to Him.

I will be a partaker of the good life here on earth for I am prosperous due to God. I am changing the world through my prayers and life. My witness is my life and people are attracted to me. My joy is the strength that protects my steps because my steps are in the Lord. I am in connection with God and my joy is accelerated to the giving of myself to others. My life is impacting. My life is the working out of the Lord.

I am content with God. I am satisfied in God. I am confident in God. God you are good to me and I hold on to you and I am delivered by you. You have taken me by the hand and you have brought me through. Lord, bless me with righteousness and riches. As I walk with you riches come because of my life walking with you. Lord I need you so I can bless others. I know that you want me to bless others and I will through you blessing me. I am an instrument of blessing for others.

I am the first fruit of God and I belong to Him. I give myself to Him daily and I am attached to the vine of the Father. I am entitled to His holiness and blessings that He has and I receive with understanding. The root in my ground is holy and all that come forth is of God. I am dedicated to the field of God and I am overturning in the promise of prosperity. I shall not be uprooted out of the ground of the Master.

I bring order to my life and this is how I develop. I am in the order of God and my blessings come to me in the timing of God. Daily my manners are laid before the Lord and God is pleased with my life. The devil will not come and still my order. The devil will not come against my seed and devour it.

I will not take the things of God and use them for myself. God is Holy and the things of God are Holy. God except me as an offering unto you. You are the principle and the promise in my life. I am in the Lord and there are no limits within God for my life. I am a manifestation of the results of the first fruit offering. I am taking the steps now to be free from debt. My goal is to be out of debt according to the Word of God. I am releasing my faith to make progress towards my financial goals and I am in covenant with God. I am entitled to be blessed. I have the faith to move whatever is blocking my bridge to the land of wealth.

I have God flowing through my life and I pour into others the life of God. Out of my belly flows the river of life. The Word of God speaks to me, through me and I move in the perfect love of Christ. I live to win people into the kingdomship of God. Through this I have received the power to love and this agape love flows through me and I am a river of the undamable love of God. Nothing can clog the love steam of God. Unto you Lord I lift up my soul today, AMEN…

DAY 14
Today I Prophecy This Pray Up-On My Life

God is my connection and I am in the position to receive. The devil can not entrap me due to the revealing light of God. God has prepared a way of escape and the ability to see from a distance the plans to devour. I thank my Lord for the ability to see in the places of God. I will not be weary in my well doing for God is pleased with me. I am in the molding hand of God and I am formed to be reformed in Him.

I am sustained by God. My destiny has been established and I prophecy to myself that I shall live and not die. I made the decision to live inside of the Lord my God. Who can touch me there, no one can. Christ lives inside of me and no weapon can form itself against me to bring me harm. It's the Christ that lives in me that stands by truth.

My life is in the place of victory and I stand in this place until He calls for me elsewhere. God moves in me until all are effected by my passing by. The rebuke of the Lord is against the mouth of every enemy. I will not continue to be knocked down by the repeating moments of the flesh. In order to stay with God I break free of those things that are not like God. I hate the things that God hates. I have made the decision to be holy before the Lord. There is no rule over my life but the ruling of God.

I am birthed out of the Holy Spirit of God unto the ministry of God. I am on the holy hill and God is showing me His greatness. Here I can hear His voice and I see His ways. Here I am renewed everyday and I am in the miracle working power of God. Here I wait on God and He rewards me there. This is where I receive my word and my massage. In this place the Word of God has been installed on the inside of me.

I pray my family out of hell and into the kingdomship of God. NOW, in the name of Jesus it is so. My life is the passageway to the Lord and I wave in all that I know and see their way into the leading of the Lord. I am the trumpet blower of my family and I sound out over the valleys that comes to separate me and the people that belong to the Lord. I will shout until they hear the guidance of the voice of the Lord that comes from within me. I come to lead my people into freedom and I turn them over to the Lord of Host. Thy hand oh Lord is upon me to win. And all that you have assigned me too, I go to war for them.

I will not hesitate to praise you. I will not hesitate to worship you. Your glory affects me in ways that my words can not explain. You define just who and what I am and I wait on you. You are the problem solver of my life. My passion for you is higher then anything that I have ever known.   I am in the timing of God and in-tuned with His Spirit. I shall not hold on to the things of death. Only my flesh shall die daily.

I give no person power over me. I will not surrender to weakness. I purge myself in the sight of God. I address temptation and I hold it responsible for its approach against me. My flesh desires to be an unbroken stallion but the Spirit of God has mounted upon the back of my flesh and brings subjection down upon it.

I sacrifice myself for a higher level in God. I realize that you are Holy. The place where you are is a place full of glory. I live with a clear mind and I will not worry. My thinking is not paralyzed because my mind is on Christ. To worry is to sin so I believe in the LORD. My thoughts are clear and my vision is the sight of God. God has not given me the spirit of fear and I rejoice in the present and the future. My enemies are at peace with me and those that stand against me fall by my side in the warfare of the Spirit.

I will live a life of happiness and wealth. I will live in the hope of the LORD. I will not worry about what I am not but be thankful for who I am. My joy is absolute and it is the strength in my sole. My garment of the LORD is seamless and made new everyday.

My life is a life of:
Prayer
Fasting
Praise
Worship

Fullness of Life
Hope and happiness in the Holy Ghost…

The blood of Jesus covers me today, AMEN…

DAY 15
Today I Prophecy This Pray Up-On My Life

Today I walk in the power of

Heaven
_____

Today I walk in the power of
_____

Giving
_____

Today I walk in the power of
_____

Goodness
_____

Today I walk in the power of
_____

Mercy
_____

Today I walk in the power of
_____

Blessings

Today I walk in the power of
_____

Hope
_____

Today I walk in the power of
_____

Prosperity
_____

Today I walk in the power of
_____

Humbleness
_____

Today I walk in the power of
_____

Peace
_____

Today I walk in the power of
_____

Successful completion
_____

Today I walk in the power of
_____

Spirit filled direction
_____

Today I walk in the power of
_____

Manifested wisdom
_____

Today I walk in the power of
_____

Devine direction
_____

Today I walk in the power of
_____

The anointing (the power to do my assignment)
_____

Today I walk in the power of
_____

Money management
_____

Today I walk in the power of
_____

Kingdom currency
_____

Today I walk in the power of
_____

Truth
_____

Today I walk in the power of
_____

Victory over principalities
_____

Today I walk in the power of
_____

Demanding prophecies bi-way of the Kingdom
_____

Today I walk in the power of
_____

A positive mouth
_____

Today I walk in the power of

_____

Faith that moves God

_____

Today I walk in the power of

_____

The passing by of thieves, muggers and robbers

_____

Today I walk in the power of

_____

Spirit filled motion, mobility and activity

_____

Today I walk in the power of

_____

My words forming God in someone's life today

_____

Today I walk in the power of

_____

Kingdom laws and regulations

_____

Today I walk in the power of

_____

Protection of heaven

_____

Today I walk in the power of

_____

Perfection

_____

Today I walk in the power of

_____

Sanctification

_____

Today I walk in the power of

_____

Excellence

_____

Today I walk in the power of

_____

Holiness

_____

Today I walk in the power of
_____

Liberty and truth
_____

Today I walk in the power of
_____

The law of God
_____

Today I walk in the power of
_____

The garment of warfare
_____

Today I walk in the power of
_____

The Spirit of God
_____

Today I walk in the power of
_____

Holy manors towards others
_____

Today I walk in the power of
_____

Courage and not fear
_____

Today I walk in the power of
_____

The prayer of my Lord
_____

Today I walk in the power of
_____

The position of receiving
_____

Today I walk in the power of
_____

Faith and wonders
_____

Today I walk in the power of
_____

A winning attitude
_____

Today I walk in the power of
___

Honesty
___

Today I walk in the power of
___

Being the last peace to someone's puzzle
___

Today I walk in the power of
___

Confidence and not worry
___

Today I walk in the power of
___

Controlling my flesh
___

Today I walk in the power of
___

The provision of God
___

Today I walk in the power of

_____

Victory

_____

Today I walk in the power of

_____

Agape love

_____

Today I walk in the power of

_____

Revelation

_____

Today I walk in the power of

_____

Joy

_____

Today I walk in the power of

_____

Fulfillment of destiny

_____

Today I walk in the power of

_____

Laughter

_____

Today I walk in the power of

_____

Loving someone other than myself

_____

Today I walk in the power of

_____

The foot steps of God

_____

Today I walk in the power of

_____

Goodness and mercy

_____

Today I walk in the power of

_____

The witness of the Lord

_____

Today I walk in the power of

_____

The presence of God

_____

Today I walk in the power of

_____

Financial genius

_____

Today I walk in the power of

_____

New wine and not brokenness

_____

Today I walk in the power of

_____

God given leadership

_____

Today I walk in the power of

_____

Being happy

_____

Today I walk in the power of

_____

Health

_____

Today I walk in the power of

_____

Good conduct

_____

Today I walk in the power of

_____

Being fearless unto accomplishment

_____

These things I speak into existence and I walk in expectation in the MATCHLESS name of Jesus Christ, Amen…

DAY 16
Today I Prophecy This Pray Up-On My Life

I take up and put on the garment of peace and I worry not. What matters to me today is that I get in contact with you LORD. I give to you the tithe of this day that you have blessed me with and I express joy in giving it too you. You are the authority in my life and my purpose is to please you today. I am in pursuit of your glory and you touch me before I leave my home today. Allow me to put my person in the place of your finding.

Today I am more than what I was yesterday. By the power of heaven my life is on a higher level today. My practice is in the things of God and I perform them over and over and over again. I stand under the umbrella of God. I enter into the tent of God. I am in the lyric of the song of worship and I sing with the voice of brokenness.

Today I move by your voice. Today I move in your Word. I give my love to those that you bring before me today. I shall not move in the lies of the world and its lustful suggestions. I answer to you God and not the laws of this world. You are my coach. You are my direction for this day. I will not be disobedient today or in the days to come. I take my steps by the tone and direction of your voice in submission to you. Authority is good and it was set up by you. I take the promises of God and I apply them to my life in fullness and completeness.

I Take and Apply This Promise to My Life

I take and apply this promise to my life
_____

He is coming in glory to reward every man according to his works
_____

I take and apply this promise to my life
_____

The establishment of his church
_____

I take and apply this promise to my life
_____

The gift of the Holy Spirit
_____

I take and apply this promise to my life
_____

The second coming and its signs
_____

I take and apply this promise to my life

___

He is sitting on the right hand of power and coming in the clouds of heaven

___

I take and apply this promise to my life

___

The signs that should follow the gift of the Holy Spirit

___

    I am going to make it today because Christ lives in me. I am safe because I live in God. I am free because the Word of God says that I am. Freedom is mine because the I AM that I AM is working within me. The reason why I am successful today is because I have put all of my trust in the Lord and He has made me glad.

    I purpose myself to tell someone today about you God. I will share my experience with you and with someone else. My words of you shall be like refreshing water to the dusty sole of those that you send me to today.

    Your Sword is at the neck of the enemy and I await your instructions unto death. The weapons from your presence are what I chose to use against the thief.

I reside in your place and I lie at your feet. I am in the now with you and I sing to you my praise. My tears are the expression of my love for you. How can I express how I feel about you? Only you can intrepid my tears and you hear the emotions of my heart.

Today my voice is the trumpet of brass before you and my hands are the fans that offer you glory. I will not be preoccupied with the things of this world only you have my heart and my ear. My passion is found hidden from all that is not of you. My passion for you is formed by all that you have done for me. You have placed your hand on me this day and I am waiting for you in the waiting place of your presence. I am hidden until you call for me then I will reveal my place only to your voice of comfort and joy. You know just where I am.

I will be in the stance of handling what may come against me today. You are my present help in trouble. Do not remove this place in my life until I learn what you have placed before me. There are places that I need to walk in for the safety of my sole. I see you in the fear and the beauty of your glory. Your beauty is found in the places of danger. The treading places possess the presence of God. You are in the place where I must go through and I am in the hand of comfort. I shall fear no evil because you are with me.

Teach me to see the beautiful things in the ugly

places that I find myself in. My situations are your situations because I give them to you. I can not fix what I'm going through I can only give them to you. This is how I praise you. This is why I worship you. This is the purpose of my warfare in the spirit.

The closing of my door is a sign to the world that you are in control of my life. My rising is managed by the Lord. The issues in my life are in the presence of God. There is no tug of war against my Father and the world. God is in control of all my confrontations and points of balance. All of my problems I give to the Lord and they are ashes in the furnace. My mind is open to the Lord and all communication is clear and I respond to Him in truth and the vehicle of love.

Today I Am

An anointed leader

_____

Today I am

_____

A winner

_____

Today I am

_____

A conqueror

_____

Today I am

_____

A possessor of the anointing to do (whatever I need)

_____

Today I am

_____

In the victory of the Lord

_____

Today I am

_____

On a level over my flesh

_____

Today I am

_____

The kiss of the Lord

_____

Today I am

_____

The embrace of the Father

_____

Today I am

_____

The scent that God desires

_____

    With respect I come before you Lord. With love and worship I bow down before you in devotion to you. I come closer in intimacy to you in the room of my Master. The anointing is taking me over, now in the place of God. The glory of the Lord is supernaturally upon me now. I am in the familiar of the Lord and the result is a miracle. Your atmosphere has arrived in my presence. It is before my face and I am bowing before my God. I prophecy these things that I have spoken upon my person now in the name of Jesus. I see it by faith before it comes. GOD will do it for me, His child in the name of Jesus.

    I shall never give up on God. I will never shy away or flinch against your promises towards me. Your mercies are endless. I will worship you forever. I will give you praise through it all. I will, I will, I will, I will give you praise. God you are never late when you come to my rescue.

Do the unheard of in my life. I speak that word now against me. **Do the unheard of in my life**, thank you. I feel the anointing of the prayer warriors of the world and Spirit unifying.

I receive those results of the prayers that come from all over the world. God will use all the hurt, stones, sickness and pain to strengthen me. I am cut form the pattern of God. I am cut from the template of the Master. I am sewn by the hand of heaven and the seams of my life are not fragile but strong. My hem is the fold and finish of faith and my garment is now finished couture (custom made) against me. In this garment I bow down in the presence of the All Mighty God. God give me the passion for your presence. I take it and I walk out into the entrances of the LORD. You are now in me in fullness of overflow and the devil recognizes my relationship with God. I have you in me now before the trouble comes. I need the level of the anointing that destroys all that is not like Him.

I walk in the awareness and the effective presence of the All Mighty God. Now in Jesus Holy name.

God is restoring all that

I lost
_____

God is restoring all that
_____

Was taken from me
_____

God is restoring all that
_____

Was stolen from me
_____

Thank You Lord, AMEN….

DAY 17
Today I Prophecy This Pray Up-On My Life

Today I am empowered by the Kingdom of heaven. Everything that God has for me is in my mouth and in my heart operating in the obedience and humbleness of my heart. The weeds that grow up to cover my path will not have success today. I will not become entangled or tripped up by there hindering ways. The Lord is the light unto my path and the power of my salvation. I my not understand everything and its methods but the Kingdom of God is assisting and working on my behalf.

I have learned to put my trust in my heavenly Father and not man. I position my behavior and response to others towards heaven so that there is no retraction missed promise or missed blessing. I attach my Kingdom of God ID on my person so that all that is trying to deny my access to where I belong today will stand aside and I will enter into the places and purpose of Gods will for me today. Nothing can stand against me today because I call on the name of Jesus.

I take my mouth and exchange it for the mouth of God. I take my character and exchange it for the character of God. Every gesture that I display towards others today will be weighted and scanned by the Word of God before I release it toward another. My goal for today is to think, speak, respond and walk holy. My God is holy so I desire to be and act holy as well.

I pray for those that are my enemies. I pray for all the hatters that would like to see me fail today. To the on lookers I speak the Kingdom up-on you today for my trust is in the Lord of host. God's ways are not our ways and my ways are not the ways of this world. I will not be tempted to enter into unholy conversations of joking that will harm others and damage my witness. I allow the Holy Spirit to speak to me with discipline and encouragement today.

I rebuke all hindering spirits and those that travel with them. I come against any doormat evil that lay at my door waiting for the weak moments in my life to over take me. All suggestions that come from the devil will not take root. I will not allow any type of reasoning to take place. I realize that the devil is the father of lies and he can not parent my mouth. I will not allow it by the power of the gospel that is salvation for those that believe. I speak this prayer along with the Word of God and it is my protection. The whole amour of God is upon me and I stand in truth and confidence.

My bible is my light, sword and shield. I am covered by the blood of the Lamb of God. This is the day that the Lord has made and I will rejoice and be glad in it. I own up to all of my faults, failures and short comings. I pause, take a deep breath and began to renew my mind with God's Word. I practice making higher levels of good decision making that could set me backward toward what I am working to receive today.

I put in my heart to develop a plain for myself going towards excellence and progress. My mind is set to move forward and not get discouraged due to what I can not control. I am setting goals in life and in ministry. Unto to the Lord I lift up my sole. Show me your ways oh Lord and teach me thy path. Lead me in your truth and help me to be truthful with myself.

I am the head and not the tail. I am patient and not found to be caught up in procrastination. This is my day and I stand firm not allowing God-less things to belittle me or hold me back from what God has given me. Point my way today Lord and show me the right way to go and give me the words to speak. I stay away from the hindrance and tempting mouth of negative people and I will not get caught up in non-productive conversations today. Bridle my tongue and bit my mouth. Let no distant beauty mislead me to commit what is holy to an unholy practice. Today my standard is firm and my measuring stick is set. I am holy and I am also the righteousness of God.

In The Mighty Name Of Jesus, Amen…

DAY 18
Today I Prophecy This Pray Up-On My Life

I worship until I feel the presence of the Lord. Today I ask for nothing of myself. This is how I worship you. Here I am to worship you. Your presence is in this place. Be exalted Lord, I came to worship you. Here I am loving you and living at your feet. I sing the songs that identify you. I bow to sing in the Spirit until I sing out of my flesh. I will present my praise and give all that I have back to you. For all that I have comes from you. Halleluiah, Halleluiah, Halleluiah, Halleluiah. Halleluiah, Halleluiah, Halleluiah, Halleluiah.

I feel you now Lord. There is no other like you. You are my functioning power and my ability to stand in the unattainable times. Others may fall but in you I will stand. While the guards change nothing will be lost. My worship is from the heart of my life. My validation is from your hand. I can not express my love for you. There is no word on this earth or under that can describe how much I love you.

I love to meet you in prayer. I will fast until my flesh falls away from me. My sole reaches out for you until I take hold of you. I desire the saturation of your anointing. I take hold of liberation in the Holy Ghost.

Your Word brings your anointing and understanding into my life. I say today that I will get personal with you. Please approve my life so you can make interaction for me. I am called to dwell near you. It is a deliberate action from me to live in the presence of God. I must dwell in the tabernacle of the Lord. You are satisfying. You have separated me to dwell around your Glory oh God. You are the power that is found in the most Holy of Holy places.

I am not in the sense of this world. I am in the knowledge of God. I am an arrow that has been pulled back within the bow of heaven. I am a servant that has been shouting towards heaven. I go up into the places of God in order to receive the Word of God and I shall be in continuance of the bow of heaven. I shall camp out in the presence of God. The Spirit has fastened its self in me and I move by the clear speech of you speaking inside of me.

I have been called to the effecting level of God. This is the place of God and He has called us unto saturation and sensitivity unto the presence of His Spirit. The Glory of God is my place of rest. The Glory of God is in the place of the sound of rain. My focus is blind to this world but clear in the sight of the Spirit. The elevation of God has come under my feet and I am lifted up with a word. This word is the word of motion and the tearing down. This sound is in my ears and translated in the words of Holiness and separation. I need to see what God has for me in the Spirit. I need to hear what God has for me in the Spirit.

I will feel the things that God has for me to become tangible within the Spirit of the Father.

I am obedient to the shifting of heaven. I am stepping into the shifting of the Spirit. I am guided and stirred into the place that God has me to be. Now, I speak it NOW in the name of Jesus. I take up the whaling of the Holy Ghost and I command my flesh to be a trained person of God.

I Am

Persistent in prayer
_____

I Am
_____

Constant in my worship
_____

I Am
_____

Determined to live in the life of my Father
_____

I Am

Relentless in my search for the touch of God

I Am

Continual in the call and response of God

I Am

The possessor of the anointing

I Am

Receiving limitless revelation

I Am

Overflowing with the power of God

I Am

The student of the Kingdom

I am under the leadership of the I Am that I Am

In Jesus, AMEN…

DAY 19
Today I Prophecy This Pray Up-On My Life

I shall fast and prayer until my flesh is subject unto the Lord. I will call out the name of Jesus until the enemy retreats in fear and trembling. I am not a coward in the spirit. I am a well trained warrior and my weapons are not carnal. The Word of God is a Sword in the Spirit. Let your alter fall before me because your alter comes from the most HolyPlace. This alter is untouched by earthly hands. This alter is a return into the wilderness place where the Ark of the Covenant Spirit dwelled. Only your chosen were aloud to touch what was Holy. This alter is not for the sinner but for the sanctified.

There is something in the name of Jesus. There is balance, power and peace. This something is unexplainable. I take this something and I feast on it. This something enables me to fight and stand in victory. I will lose nothing with you on my side. When Jesus is for me then who can be against me.

I will pray with specific terminology and I will trust in the direction of my prayer. The peace that passes all understanding has not passed me. I am guarded by the peace of God.

I will not be possessed by the evil of this world. Evil has to become subject to the Word Himself,

Jesus. The Lord is my master and every tongue will confess this truth. God is my deliverer and the unclean cannot place anything within my garment. I will not be tormented by the enemy. Unto the Lord my sole is lifted and protected by God. My inner man responds only in trust to my Savior. My agreement is in the Lord.

I will not be with out Gods' will. I will take my assignment today and cloth my today with the victory that is in God. My righteousness opens many doors. I wheel the will of God. I bow down and ask of you to make your will in me pure. I uphold your will as a banner and I run and it flies in the breath of your wind. This obedience towards you Lord teaches the onlooker to live in your will for themselves.

The law of this world is not the law of God. The world lies and tries to form weapons to come against me. The things that are not good for me I will not accept them. When the world comes to me I repeat my commitment unto you. I am the image of you God and I am in pursuit of you. I long to show you God just how much I love you and adore you. There is nothing like you and nothing can compare to you. I will speak the words of Job "I will never speak against you LORD". When I am in trouble I worship and the angles of God react in protection for me and my family.

I will bless you LORD at all times and your

praise and song shall always be in my house. Through my praise the hands that I lift are anointed. With my mouth I lift you and my lifting brings the power forth from my mouth. With my heart I hold you and the Spirit of your agape love takes over all anger, fear and revenge that come to sit and fester within me. I lift up my head and shout through the sky that I belong to you.

From The Book of Psalms:

Today your word is a lamp unto my feet, and a light unto my path

___

Today the entrance of your words gives me light

___

Today the light of the righteous rejoice: but the lamp of the wicked shall be put out.

___

You LORD have called me in righteousness, and you will hold my hand, and will keep me, and give me for a covenant of the people, for a light of the Gentiles;

___

You are my hope, O Lord GOD

___

Uphold me according to your Word that I may live: and let me not be ashamed of my hope

---

Therefore my heart is glad, and my glory rejoice: my flesh also shall rest in hope

---

But you are He that took me out of the womb: and my hope is in you

---

In you, O LORD, do I hope: you will hear me, O Lord my God.

    LORD, today I wave to you to get your attention. Look my way today because I am dancing only for you. I blow kisses and then laugh because my love for you makes me do things that make people frown in misunderstanding. I dangle my praise before you and I call your name for you to come and take it. I am in the position to leap out and catch you when you come by. Please come now so we can talk. Come before I began to cry. If so, may my tears be a voice the causes you to stand still and behold just how much I'm in love with you. You are my passion. You are my hope and my light. You are my water. You are my breath of life. You are my flower and my sunshine. You are the ocean that I hear. You are the peace that comforts me and no other god will I hear. My offering is only to you. I need to be in a time of intimacy with you. I'm only saying that God, I love you.

In the matchless name of the Father
The Son and the Holy Ghost. AMEN…

DAY 20
Today I Prophecy This Pray Up-On My Life

The seed of prayer is what I plant today in the world. I am not seeding by myself but the prayer warriors around the world are planting at this time. I pray fervently and powerful with the passion of heaven. All walls, structures and plans that are coming towards me are shattered by the shattering power of God. God has strengthened my places of vulnerability. Now, they are only places of victory in me. God makes strong my places of weakness.

The striking place of the enemy is revealed to me through the revelation of God. I pray with the prayer of faith against those things that come against my confidence. I am positioned in heavenly places. The Holy Ghost has come upon me and I have help and power to do anything in the will of God. LORD I am the righteous and you deliver me out of all of my trouble. I am covered by the blood and I am in the position of victory today. I have help in Jesus today.

I bind on the earth while God binds in heaven and I see the proof of this power to bind. The devil can not pull me away from God. The devil is a liar I am the righteousness of God. I call on the Word and He speaks Himself upon me. The warriors are more then one and we put the enemies to flight. Lord you are my strong tower today. You are my battleaxe in the times of war. The battle belongs to God. It is not mine but the Lords.

I pray with persistence. I pray with power. I pray in the relationship of the prayer wheel. I pray with purpose and precision. When I go through my darkest hour you oh Lord are my light.

The flesh is a weak place so I go up in the spirit where the Spirit of the Lord is and it is a powerful place in God. The fleshly place is a place of the earth. My wrestling place is in the place of the Spirit and I fight there. I want the flame of the Spirit, a new place of prayer. I leave myself, my spirit and God will be where He desires me to go.

Today you make the crooked places straight. I need you today more than yesterday. Revive me. Refresh me today oh Lord and I will say yes to you all the day long in my spirit. I need you Lord to help me today. Out of my mouth is yes all day. I shout help until you deliver me.

I will thank the Lord and praise Him at all times and I will praise you all day in my person. God you are my reason for praise. Your Word gives me joy and motivation. I tape into your well that flows from the depth of my belly. I need to drink of you and then I will be satisfied until I thirst again. Keep my flesh thirsty for you. Keep my spirit thirsty for you. My sole is thirsting now oh God and I come out of myself today. I will cry out to you until I receive your power from heaven. I will cry out until all my pain is gone. I will cry out to you until you touch me and I can stand in your presence.

I travail and push forth a new language and place in you. I will press until I come to the place that is in you. I continue in the groaning that can not be uttered and I mown until I break through the place of groaning. I holler out until I feel the fire of heaven fall upon me. I'm pushing. I'm pressing. I'm in the birth position and I push until I hear my blessing cry out. This is the time to go where no other may have ever gone before. Take me there oh Lord.

The Lord trains me in His Spirit. Allow me to grow in you. Let not the final come to me until I finalize all things with you in completion and you are satisfied with my life. When I die I live. I need you to be satisfied with me. I need you to be pleased with me. I shall see your face in peace. You are the fulfillment of my life and I will see you in peace. I long to hold you and speak to you from my heart everyday. You are the satisfaction in my sole.

I am living the life that you God have willed for me. I will never be satisfied until I connect with you. Seal the Word of revelation in me. Wake up any dormancy and pronounce your blessing upon me.

Place inside of me a door knocking boldness unto entry. For I am yours and I desire to be used by you.

Amen…

DAY 21
Today I Prophecy This Pray Up-On My Life

I prophecy inside of this power. There, the Lord is liberty and I move in the prophetic timing of God. Wake up the gifts that you have placed inside of me as my faith increase and my life produces. Pronounce the supernatural revelation up-on my life. Give me the Spirit of wisdom to come forth like the wind into my existence. Seed my womb and cause a welling to break forth from my belly and burden me to call on the name of Jesus in Spirit filled language.

This cry from within my womb speaks to every nation. Releasing those that are captured and held in captivity in their flesh. To those that are unable to minister and to those that cannot break free I loose them now by the authority in Jesus Christ.

To be pleasing to the Lord I submit my being and become a servant to Christ. Overthrowing the options of society I submit unto the flowing increase of God. I come inline with your order and I take freedom to be set free and I live in the seasons of being loosed. I serve in the reign of you Lord my master. This prayer, I prophetically speak these words upon myself. God do something different in my life today I pray. Bring revival to my being. Open what has been closed to me. Continue to stir me and affect my super natural until I prophecy the renewing upon my entire being.

I welcome your voice. I raise up your standard with my life being a banner unto your praise. I reach for you and take hold of you. I embrace my calling that you have feed through my lips that my belly shall not return. I shall move in the saving move of God calling out those things that hold back and tear down. And I join intercessors all over the world and I continue to affect the realms within the spirit until.

As I prophecy on earth the Lord has spoken it in heaven. God I want to tell you that I love you without measure. I speak to you in the Spirit because earthly words cannot express how I fell about you. Lord, release me from the post of this world and direct me unto your path. Right now I prophecy that there is purpose happening for me from you. Dismantle all things that are not like you. Where am I to stand when you shift? I will move when you move. Place me in the womb of your Spirit. God I need an encounter with you. When my prayer leaves from earth my answer descends from heaven. Heavens pregnancy is now within me.

Bring your anointing Lord upon the whole earth. Desend down on me now and lock your will deep inside me causing me to intercede and cry out until you hear. I speak to the principalities, earthly authorities and all other forms of legalism to fall down before my God. Allow your glory to over shadow the earth and lay at my hands your law. Return into the schools, return into politics and reenter every area that man has built. Tare down and rebuild for your Glory.

I prophecy against the cities, states and the nations that all doors swing open to your will. Open oh Lord the doors to all institutions and anoint all officers and officials to do the work of the Lord. Bring the kingdoms of the world to the place of worshiping you. Let the lust of the world be disabled and you release your ability to break free.

I release your seeds of prophecy and prayer in the realm of this day and time. I come into your place Lord until change comes upon me.

I prophecy to my heart that its passion is only towards you. This panting that I feel is because of my love for you. I speak peace to noise, comfort, peace and silence to disturbance. I'm broken unto trusting you. I need to be in a relationship of trust with you Lord.

I rebuke all pride that I may have today. I bit my mouth and hand the reigns to you. Guide me all the way home where you are. I resist all things that are not like you. I possess the power of the anointing so strong that the filling up of God empties out on the sick and they are healed daily.

Amen…

DAY 22
Today I Prophecy This Pray Up-On My Life

Today I walk in faith and perfect health. I will have faith in God because I say to the mountains of today move out of my way. I shall not doubt in my heart that what I speak by the name of the Lord, as long as it is His will, I shall have it. I don't care what people say or what people do. I shall have what I speak in the Lord. I use the faith that the Lord has given me and I develop my faith to be on a higher level. My faith is in use and functional in my belief in the Word of God. All I need is time in the presence of God and I can do all things through Christ Jesus because He is my strength.

My faith is in action and I speak it in aim towards the mountains today. I believe it and I act on it until it comes forth. I believe God for the needs of my life and I'm moving forward and I possess it now through my action.

God you have a plan for my life and I have the faith to carry it out. Daily I face the foul things of this world but I take the time now to worship while the angles are my protection for today sent from you. Now I pray this prayer of faith through my life and I move mountains today out of my path. To give up is not an option. I will not give in to the devil today. There is no intimidation factor that can keep me from you God. No one can stand against you and win.

Today I will work my job like I am a child of God. Today my boss will be blessed because I am in their presence. I will honor the Lord while I'm eating my lunch and I am searching for a soul to encourage. My heart is prepared for kindness towards others today. I will not be an angry person. I will not have the desire to punish others in revenge today. I will be quick to forgive, to respond and react in love.

I am building up in my

Faith today

_____

I am building up in my

_____

Love today

_____

I am building up in my

_____

Companionship today

_____

I am building up in my

_____

Holy sanctified style of life today

I am in the Lord all the day long.

    I will face my fears with the confidence of the Lord. And He shall take all of my fears away. I am emotionally available to you Lord. This is an opportunity to show myself to you today. I have a lot to give and I give it all to you in worship. I know that you see me in all that I do and you have been just with me. I need to be in a place where I can talk and share with you.

    Lord fix me and make me whole today. I am your child and I want to be an obedient child in you. I need you to be an implosion in me taking out all that you dislike about me.

    I will not walk in ungodliness today. I will not push away the truth nor will I push it down. I will not be in the position of evil in no way today. I will see your creation and not mans destruction of day. Today I will live in the totality and centricity of your Glory. I long to see in the invisible and abide where you are. Allow my prayer to be a sweet smell in your presence.

    I am listening for what the Spirit is saying to me. I know that you are talking to my entire being and

I'm listening for you. Lord, create a workshop just for me where I can come and you lay your hands upon me. I need you to work on me today and everyday in everyway. I surrender to you and I lay before you. The Spirit of God is the specialist that I need to bring an answer to my difficulties. God you are my doctor and my lawyer. Today you are everything that I need for my life and for this day. Restore the years of my life that I wasted and/or misused.

I Exchange My

Ashes for your beauty

_____

I exchange my

_____

Mistakes of your direction

_____

I exchange my

_____

Disaster for your rescue

_____

I exchange my

_____

Time for your eternity

_____

I exchange my

_____

Labor for your fruit

_____

I exchange my

_____

Addition for your multiplication

_____

I exchange my

_____

Stubbornness for you kindness

_____

I exchange my

_____

Restlessness for your restoration

_____

I exchange my

_____

Emptiness for your Fullness
_____

I exchange my
_____

Lowness for your higher level
_____

I exchange my
_____

No for your yes
_____

I exchange my
_____

Declination for your inclination
_____

I exchange my
_____

Backwardness for your forwardness
_____

I exchange my
_____

Downward thoughts for your upstanding truth

___

I exchange my

___

Uneventfulness for your miracles

___

I exchange my

___

Reputation for your name

___

I exchange my

___

Entanglement for your undoing

___

I exchange my

___

Single actions for your partnership

___

I exchange my

___

Stressed life for your relaxation

_____

I exchange my

_____

Response for your response

_____

I exchange my

_____

Past for your future

_____

I exchange my

_____

Misunderstanding for your understanding

_____

I exchange my

_____

Fear for your confidence

_____

I exchange my

_____

Hesitance for your reaction

_____

I exchange my

_____

Ways for your ways

_____

I exchange my

_____

Hate for your love

_____

I exchange my

_____

Foresight for your vision

_____

I exchange my

_____

Knowledge for your wisdom

_____

I exchange my

_____

Lyric for your song
___

I exchange my
___

Habitual lifestyle for your unfailing love
___

    My trust is in you and I exchange my life for your death in order so that I can live.

AMEN and AMEN…

DAY 23
Today I Prophecy This Pray Up-On My Life

I pray to you oh Lord my Father who lives in heaven, Holy is your name your kingdom come. Your will be done in earth, as it is in heaven. Give me this day my daily bread. And forgive me my debts, as I forgive my debtors. And lead me not into temptation, but deliver me from evil for thine is the kingdom, and the power, and the glory, for ever. Amen.

I am a seed that you have planted in the ground. I lift my hands until you water me. I am a tree that has developed through the places of time. My hands are lifted up only to you asking for you to rain on me. You have placed me a as tree, and my roots are planted by the rivers of living waters.

I am in your ground and nothing can pluck me out of your hands. I am a seed for the world and I am sown in good ground. I practice seed sowing principles and I understand the law of the seed. I sow and I release my seed of faith into the entire world and it dies in the ground.

Miracles happen now by the faith of your wisdom sowing in the earth. You have a harvest that is coming now into my life. My faith is a seed. My time is a seed. God when I ask for a harvest you will ask me for a seed. And I shall release my seed of faith and it shall activate unto me. My harvest comes as a result of a seed. I will not hold this seed without releasing it into the ground of return.

I am in the position of seed time and harvest. Today I shall plant in the ministry of the Father. I am working the ground that my father has assigned me to. Whichever way my seed investment can be used today I give my time, my money and my opportunity to you today. Use it as you will.

I Sow a Seed For:

Financial freedom
_____

I sow a seed for
_____

Total physical health
_____

I sow a seed for
_____

Reconnection with my family
_____

I sow a seed for
_____

Great spiritual strength
_____

I sow a seed for
_____

Productive living
_____

I sow a seed for
_____

The wisdom to lead soles to Christ
_____

I sow a seed for
_____

Continual seed and harvest
_____

 I sow a seed for
_____

My pastor and his family
_____

    LORD you will bless me, and in multiplication you will multiply my seed as the stars of the heaven and as the sand which is upon the sea shore; and thy seed shall possess the gates of my enemies.

My seed is multiplying now with great blessing. AMEN…

DAY 24
Today I Prophecy This Pray Up-On My Life

I shall be productive today and I shall do it with simplicity. I will use the principles of yea and nea. Today I will take out time for me and God. I will show love today and change the things that I need to change. I will not walk around with a bad attitude today. I will unmask all that is hiding in me. I will not be deceived by the enemy today or become tangled in his mess. Today will be a GREAT day.

Today God I serve you with my whole heart. My mouth shall be found in the Lord. Today I will not walk the path of poison but I will run towards the presence of God. Today my laughter is in the joy of the Lord and in Him I am satisfied. If I become confused within my day I will look to the Lord and my focus shall return quickly and sure.

Following people is not the wisdom of God I will follow the Lord and I am happy. Today I will clean my home my car and all other things that the Lord has blessed me with. I will take care of the things that God has blessed me to have.

I will pray in the anointing. I will call you Lord and I know that you will answer. The things that I see today will be in my prayer to the Lord. My day is the place of the Lord. I will not overcomplicate my day.

You God are not a God of confusion. I will not try to figure out the moving of God in my today I will just move in Him until all that is not like Him falls from me.

God alone can make my day a great day. My today is in the Lord. I have overcome this world by my days being found in the Lord. I will learn of You God and not myself. I am confident in you. I know and recognize you and I leave all in your hands. I have no will to operate in the mind of my flesh. I operate in the operational ability of my Father.

Today I am fruitful and God I live in you. And in Christ I can do all things. Apart from you oh Lord I can do nothing. I am anxious for you and I depend totally on you. God you have to be in my plans. Better yet my plans are in you. You are on my side and I laugh at all that come to challenge me. For when they challenge me they take on all of heaven. Within myself is the great I AM. You teach and I will learn. I will not worry for to worry is to sin. You are my trust and I reason not.

Today with your power I stand and I draw my weapon against the world. The armor of the Lord is on my person and I fight covered in the blood. Lord you are my best friend and I want to come over to your house everyday. I run when I hear your voice. I am ready to spend time with you in the places that you know we love to meet. Where are the promises that I am in reach of? My place is in your presence. I just love to be with you.

I am in total faith and trust in you. I acknowledge you and I leave my life in your hand. I operate in the mind of the Spirit and I am thinking in the thought of the Holy Ghost. I trust you oh Lord for my answers and I look not to the ways of the world for my response. Confusion is not from you and I do not worry because I trust you God.

All of my situations work themselves out in the Lord and I am secure there. I perform well. I am a Christian on my job and at home. Everywhere that I go I take you God with me. All of my faults are at the feet of Jesus and I will not pick them up ever again. The standards for righteousness are in my heart and I feel the beating of it.

I know who I am in you Christ my Lord because I lay before you daily asking for you to work on me. I follow the will of God for my life. God you have given me the grace to do what you have assigned me to do. I am not obedient to the law of lust but I am faithful to you my Lord. I am not self righteous instead I am the righteousness of God.

I hold to my confession in the Lord through temptation and the time of lifestyle. I receive from

God the ability to stand worthy and valuable. I press on towards the mark and the higher calling of God. God, what do I say today to those that are in need of a word from you? I shall wait in belief that you will come and give me just what I need. God I love you and you love me. You hate sin and I hate sin. God you are Holy and when you come down all things that are around you becomes Holy.

God I come boldly into your presence and I ask for the things that I need and want. I need to receive from you health, love, and favor solely form the kingdom and peace. I will praise you and worship you because I know that you will hear me. I am confident with my asking because I am in Christ.

I am enjoying you Lord in my ups and in my down times. My habits are running to you. I agree with your every Word and I refuse to speak against you. You are above my ways and my thoughts. I hold your hand when I'm unsure and in dark places. I am in the inherited place of heaven and in the timing of God and I will receive my birthright.

Nothing will steal my peace for today and joy is all day long in Jesus name, Amen.

DAY 25

DAY 25
Today I Prophecy This Pray Up-On My Life

Contentment is my garment for today. I rest within the encounter of God. My balance is steady by the steadiness of the Word and the stability of my faith. Underneath my flesh is the place of the Spirit and I live a consecrated life.

The Greater the sacrifice is the greater the reward is for me. Lord I will go through the ruff times because I know that you are with me. I place demand on what is mine to come to my house and I shall honor you. I demand my help to come by the strength of my God. Cause the overflow to come in the places of dryness and I will praise you out of my flesh.

The impression of heaven is upon me. The stamp of God is on my person. When I seek your face and I'm in your presence I become more like you. I am changed when I see your face. Like Moses Lord I desire to see you in your Glory. I know that you are too powerful to appear to my flesh but I desire to know you. I pray the Word of knowledge up-on me. I pray the great anointing upon me now right where I am.

I love you Lord in a great way. You have touched my life in a way that I can not place words upon. You are my trusting friend and no one can ever separate us. If anyone speaks lies about us I leave in a hurry while

I praise you. The enemy comes to break us apart but the love between us is too mighty.

This day I sing the song of power and love that I aim towards you. You're concerned about me and I take that and form my song that I sing to you. I am linked to you. I am coupled with you. I am associated with you and all that surrounds you.

Speak to my church Spirit of God. Teach this vessel until the river flows from my belly. Prepare me oh Lord for the war that is here today. Take me now and teach me now in your most Holy place. I need to be where your power is. I need to be where you are. My desire is in you and I am thirsty to drink of your greatness.

I speak the manifested power of Gods Spirit running towards me to overwhelm me. It is an overtaking power and I bow to receive it. Lord I want to be in your Spirit on your day. I am looking for miracles in the Spirit. I am a vehicle open for you please ride in me. I ask Lord if I can be the one that is chosen by you to go and carry your Word.

I am blessed and I am not limited in nothing. I am in victory not in defeat. You are my pass, present and my future. And in you all around me is might and power. I am going to be what you will me to be and I shall be a winner all day long. Lord I love you, I love you, I love you and the love that I have for you is real.

Lord I love your mind because you are always thinking of me. Lord I love your eyes because you use them to look upon me. With your nose you are satisfied with my praise. I love your mouth for with your Word you have shaped me.

I give to you by using my faith and not only my emotions. What I give will come back to me. I am in the spirit of process and I am in it until the end. God has a plan for me, a special assignment. I am persevered in dedication and duty and God is with me.

I saturate my heart with the Word of God and I go through what I need to in order for my day to be a success. My success is in the Lord. The Word has watered me and I can make it through by the Word of God. Only the Word can produce a successful life for me. I act on the Word of God.

I am a doer of the Word and my person follows on the order of God. I will stretch to give. God I will give my sacrifice and you will show up.

I will not give room to the devil today for him to move in my day. I will not sin in anger. I will not give the enemy any opportunity in my day today. I am slow to anger and I forsake all wrath. I will not covet someone else's belongings I am content with what the

Lord has blessed me with. My sole is satisfied in you Lord and I am joyful always. You are the penetration of joyful song in my life. I am a winner today as I leave my home and I shall return with favor and peace following me.

I desire the power of God to be the passion of my days. I am not in the wilderness of nothing but I am bending over drinking at the fountain of life. I am not in the state of mind of deserted things because I know that you are here in my mind. If I can not praise you I can not win. With my mind I will hold you up with the thoughts that are Holy. I will praise you when I am sick or in trouble. I will worship you oh my Lord when nothing seems to be working out for me. You are my leaning post and my only action towards my enemies is to come to you in worship and all other weapons of heaven.

You Are My

Promotion

_____

You Are My

_____

Endorsement

_____

You Are My

___

Help

___

You Are My

___

Support

___

You Are My

___

Sponsorship

___

You Are My

___

Back-up

___

You Are My

___

Backing

___

You Are My

Spokesman

You Are My Everything

Most righteous God, AMEN…

DAY 26

DAY 26
Today I Prophecy This Pray Up-On My Life

Lord, I speak and stretch myself in my giving today. I will give until you become my source unto my return for me to give again. The outcome of my giving is foretold in your Word.

I Will Give According To My

Righteousness
_____

I Will Give According To My
_____

Faith
_____

I Will Give According To My
_____

Word from God
_____

I Will Give According To My
_____

Burden

_____

I Will Give According To My

_____

Location

_____

I Will Give According To My

_____

Source

_____

I Will Give According To My

_____

Servitude

_____

I Will Give According To My

_____

Desire

_____

I Will Give According To My

_____

Devotion
_____

I Will Give According To My
_____

Need
_____

I Will Give According To My
_____

Harvest
_____

I will give on earth until I am translated and transformed unto the likeness of the Lord. Today I will receive from the law and promise of the first fruit offerings.

First Fruit Offerings

1) The flow of abundance with the ability to bless
2) Takes away the ability for my enemy to hurt me
3) He will expand my land holdings
4) He will make room for me at the top
5) He will place blessings on my house
6) What I have left He will consecrate even more
7) Offerings bring a supernatural supply from the kingdom

I am prepared to receive by faith. I surround myself with positive people today and not negative people. I am in the company of mountain people, people of strength, people of power, people of destiny, people of vision and people of love.

God I desire to see you clearly. I declare that all that I see today is in the plain of God. I can have all that I see because I'm blessed to see in the things of the Spirit. The needs that I have today are in the Spirit and I see them. They are at my hand and I reach for them and grab them in the name of Jesus. The future is mine and I see it. I can walk in my future because my faith gives me the power to see what God has for me and I grab it today.

I am a person of revelation and truth in the Lord. I will not be in the place of jealousy I will move and thrive in my joy. I will not move out if my place of joy for the Word of the Lord is stapled against me. Nothing will pull me down from my place. My day has a purpose for me and my day is secure. My behavior is in the Lord.

The things of the world are not the extension of my life. I am validated by the mark of the kingdom. Today I am in the promotion of God.

Today I plead the blood of Jesus over my entire family and all other people that the Holy Ghost brings to me. When I plead the blood all things that are against me has to pass me by because I am covered in the blood. I trail in the blood. My footsteps leave a trial for those that need to find my Lord but the enemy cannot follow me.

Today I sentence my flesh into death and I have chosen to live in the Lord all day. I am in the place of connection and on a higher level today in the Spirit. I am not abiding in the grave of going no where. I honor the King of Kings and I am grateful to you for pulling me out of those no where places. You are the King of Kings and the Lord of Lords and I thank you God for all that you have done.

I apply the principles of the scriptures in my life today. This is how I level the quality of my life. I am only a steward and I understand that it is all Gods. The enemy will not enslave me with debt. I will not be in denial. I will confront my problems and my shortage

I will not be in the mode of selfishness today. I will pray using the Word of God. The scripture shall be my peace His Word is like, ahhhhh – to me. I love God and no one can shake my trust in Him. Today I walk in the things that bring me closer to you God. I walk in the promises of God. Today I walk in the revelation of the wisdom and the knowledge of God. I am a producer of things that are Holy

Today I will stand fast therefore in the liberty where you oh Lord have made me free, and I am not entangled again with the yoke of bondage. I will walk in the Spirit, and I shall not fulfil the lust of the flesh today. I am led of the Spirit, and I am not under the law.

Now the works of the flesh will not manifest themselves in me, which are these:

Adultery

_____

Fornication

_____

Uncleanness

_____

Lasciviousness

_____

Idolatry

_____

Witchcraft

_____

Hatred

_____

Variance

_____

Emulations

_____

Wrath

_____

Strife

_____

Seditions

_____

Heresies

_____

Envyings

_____

Murders

_____

Drunkenness

_____

Revellings

_____

And such like

But Today I Will Function in the Fruit of the Spirit which Is:

Love
_____

Joy
_____

Peace
_____

Longsuffering
_____

Gentleness
_____

Goodness
_____

Faith
_____

Meekness
_____

Temperance

Against such there is no law. I will live in the Spirit, and also walk in the Spirit. I will not want vain glory, provoking one another or envying anything today.

With smiles of Lord filled joy, Amen…

DAY 27
Today I Prophecy This Pray Up-On My Life

My today will be better than my yesterday. My day has been moved to a place of intensity in the Spirit. I am established in the kingdom and my day is in the established. The solution for my life today is to allow my day to be recognized in the work of the Lord. I will not reject God I will rework the will of God daily. On and on I will.

You oh Lord, want me to increase so the resource that you bless me with will be sown into others. You wish above all things that I may prosper and be in good health, even as my soul prospers. Lord you are magnified and I long to be pleasurable to you. The wealth of the sinner is laid up for me. I fear the Lord and I am blessed, and I delight greatly in your commandments. Lord it is you that give me the power to get wealth and your covenant which was swore to my fathers belong to me. As it is this day.

You have come, Lord that I might have life more abundantly. I have been redeemed from the curse of the law. Your law oh Lord shall not depart out of my mouth. I shall meditate on your Word day and night. And I will to do all that is in your Word for you shall make my way prosperous, and I shall have good success. I pray this prayer upon my life today placing myself in the promise filled scripture.

Deuteronomy 28:1-2
And it shall come to pass, if thou shalt hearken diligently unto the voice of the Lord thy God, to observe and to do all His commandments which I command thee this day, that the Lord thy God will set thee on high above all nations on the earth. And all these blessings shall come on thee, and over take thee, if thou shalt hearken unto the voice of the Lord thy God.

Proverbs 24:5
A wise man is strong; yea, a man of knowledge increaseth strength.

Proverbs 4:7
Wisdom is the principal thing; therefore get wisdom: and with all thy getting get understanding.

Proverbs 3:13-18
Happy [is] the man [that] findeth wisdom, and the man [that] getteth understanding. For the merchandise of it [is] better than the merchandise of silver, and the gain thereof than fine gold. She [is] more precious than rubies: and all the things thou canst desire are not to be compared unto her. Length of days is in her right hand; [and] in her left hand riches and honour. Her ways are ways of pleasantness, and all her paths are peace. She is a tree of life to them that lay hold upon her: and happy is every one that retaineth her.

Mark 11:23-24
For verily I say unto you, That whosoever shall say unto this mountain, Be thou removed, and be thou cast into the sea; and shall not doubt in his heart, but shall believe that those things which he saith shall come to pass; he shall have whatsoever he saith. Therefore I say unto you, what things soever ye desire, when ye pray, believe that ye receive [them], and ye shall have [them].

Proverbs 18:21
Death and life [are] in the power of the tongue: and they that love it shall eat the fruit thereof.

Proverbs 23:7
For as he thinketh in his heart, so [is] he:

Proverbs 22:29
Seest thou a man diligent in his business? He shall stand before kings; he shall not stand before mean [men].

Habakkuk 2:2
And the LORD answered me, and said, write the vision, and make [it] plain upon tables, that he may run that readeth it.

2 Corinthians 5:7
For we walk by faith, not by sight:

Mark 11:24
Therefore I say unto you, what things soever ye desire, when ye pray, believe that ye receive [them], and ye shall have [them].

Romans 10:17
So then faith [cometh] by hearing, and hearing by the word of God.

Luke 6:38
Give, and it shall be given unto you; good measure, pressed down, and shaken together, and running over, shall men give into your bosom. For with the same measure that ye mete withal it shall be measured to you again.

I Believe, I Speak and I receive, doing everything that I have spoken in Jesus name, Amen.

This Is My New Way Day

My short term and long term goals are in the Lord

_____

I am in celebration

_____

Mission statement

_____

Vision statement
_____

Purpose statement
_____

Workshops
_____

Radicalism
_____

I will be _____ (fill in the blank)
_____

This is my year
_____

This is my day
_____

Plan events
_____

Plan a vacation
_____

Go visit a spa
_____

Cook an exotic meal
___

Attend a seminar
___

Bring my body into agreement with health
___

Get a vision
___

Move away from negative people
___

Practice first fruit
___

And so on and so on and so on…
___

Today I start planning my life on a higher level…

DAY 28
Today I Prophecy This Pray Up-On My Life

Today I prophecy this prayer upon my life. My Lord I speak the anointed ability up-on myself to build wealth for the purpose of the kingdom. I speak those things that are not as though they where. I am faithful in my temptation. Today I choose faith instead of failing fear. I have rights to the kingdom things that my God possess. My life, my today life rebukes the devil. I am the righteous and I cry out to the Lord and He will deliver me. God whatever it is that is being done in my life, it may look like I'm loosing but you are preparing me for the win. You are working it out in me.

I reflect on you and I am satisfied with not looking back. I am sent to the nations and I operate in the Spirit of God. I am not out of Christ but I am in Christ Jesus my Lord and savior. Today I take a higher ground and I make an arrest on all that comes against me this day. I respond to the workings of the Spirit and I am not confined in any way. This is a day of manifestation and I am a holy influence over this day and world. My city is in the radical move of God and the over shadowing of His wings are over me.

This is the day of the people of God and I will not run in hiding but in worship falling face down to the ground before you. God I need you to wash me in the power of agreement with you. Your voice is in my mouth and your Word is on my lips. I am a distribution center for the kingdom and those that are in need I will give though you. Unity has come and I position myself with all that are in tune with the body of Christ. This is a day of remnant. This is a day of power. This is a time that you Lord will make my day and victory come to pass.

I am one with you Lord and I am in love with you. I am precious to you because I love you first and foremost. I love you more than anyone else. I am cast in the light of the Master and I make a choice to be in the Glory of Christ. I am in the place of connection and I am in my place in GOD. I hear you calling me and I pause to humble myself and listen to do your will.

I live in my obedience to you and I hear your voice and I listen. My love for you Lord is not a pondering though. I know that you died for me and you love me with more then I can imagine. I love you this day oh God I will not delay my place in you. I am not alone in the presence of God. I may feel alone on earth but you are with me. Even if I can not hear you I know that you are with me. If I can't feel you I will not worry because I know that you are here.

Your shadow is on me and over me and this shadow will heal who passes by. I move today in your power. The miracles are working now and I move in them. The power to heal is all over me and I am delivered from sickness and I will speak out of my mouth the testimonies of my Lord. God you have given me the power to heal all that come for a healing. You said, "Is there any sick amount you"? I move in this question now for I am the righteousness of God and I live a holy life. I am able to speak to sickness and it will obey the Word of God. The power of the enemy is broken at the feet of you Lord. All things bow at the mention of your name. My faith is in the high places of God and I shout prophetical healing through out the earth.

Lord I shall talk about you during my day as I come in contact with others. You are making all my impossibilities possible. I have an urgency to fulfill your plan and purpose. I shall pray, give and fast until I find my place alone with you. I will do what I need to do in order to get to the place that I need to come to in God today. I am looking for results and reward in you today. I will spring forth speedily and with power coming out of the places of hindrance. I shall tap into the source of power that will restore what I have come short in. Restore inward oh God giving me exceeding grace and authority.

All things today shall respond to the voice of you God. I shall give birth to decisions that produce and I will live in wealth knowing that wealth is not money alone. You have opened my womb unto great destiny. I am going beyond any thought that I've ever had. My mind is beyond my fleshly extension. I am in the birth position and now I push in the Spirit.

Today I have come into the revelation of who I am in you. I am in you Christ and Christ you are in me. Therefore, whatever comes to hinder me I point to you and it bows in submission. Whatever is mine must respond to my speaking. Out of my mouth is your responding Word. I have dominion over my today by the word that comes out of my mouth. My words direct my day and my words are your Word.

My Decision Today Is To

Trust you

___

My decision today is to

___

Believe in you

___

My decision today is to

___

Pronounce destiny on my self

My decision today is to
___

Meet the need of my calling
___

My decision today is to
___

To expose the things that is not like you
___

My decision today is to
___

Crucify my flesh and die daily
___

My decision today is to
___

Over come pitfalls
___

              Today I Define Myself As
___

Free
___

Today I define myself as

_____

A product of you

_____

My Decision Today Is To

_____

Function righteously

_____

My decision today is to

_____

Speak purposeful

_____

My decision today is to

_____

Deliver

_____

My decision today is to

_____

Be mindful

_____

My decision today is to

_____

Desire forward mobility

_____

My decision today is to

_____

Be a pursuer of good things

_____

My decision today is to

_____

Be a possessor of a sensational life

_____

My decision today is to

_____

Be a mountain mover

_____

My decision today is to

_____

Be a servant of God

_____

My decision today is to

_____

Be a giver

_____

My decision today is to

_____

Speak life and not death

_____

My decision today is to

_____

Be a person of foresight

_____

My decision today is to

_____

Be a person of destiny

_____

My decision today is to

_____

Be a gift to the world

_____

My decision today is to

_____

Be an atmospheric influential person

_____

My decision today is to

_____

Be a person of confidence

_____

My decision today is to

_____

Be a person of opportunity

_____

My decision today is to

_____

Be a preparer of greatness

_____

My decision today is to

_____

Be a person of God

_____

My decision for today is to serve you God in the Spirit of Holiness.

AMEN.
AMEN..
AMEN…

DAY 29
Today I Prophecy This Pray Up-On My Life

Lord I cherish the process of falling in love with you today. My objective is to intensify our moments in time and our total relationship. Unemotional events are cast far away from us not connecting because I will cry out before the world that I love you. I will climb the highest mountain and tell the world that I love you more than anything. I am not ashamed to be seen with you. I will spend the time in detail description and telling you how you've inspired me to come closer.

You

Excite me

_____

You

_____

Stimulate me

_____

You

_____

Enthuse me

_____

You

___

Animate me

___

You

___

Motivate me

___

You

___

Electrify me

___

You

___

Incite me

___

You

___

Delight me

___

You
_____

Pleasure me
_____

You
_____

Bring me to bliss
_____

You
_____

Provoke me
_____

You
_____

Inflame me
_____

You
_____

Stir me
_____

You

___

Arouse me

___

You

___

Delight me

___

You

___

Bring me to gladness

___

You

___

Usher joy against me

___

You

___

Transport holy experience towards me

___

You

Bring gaze of hesitation

You

Bring sunrise

You

Bring horizon

You

Scoop my heart

You

Wheel passion

You

___

Bring intimacy

___

You

___

Cause me to run until I get free

___

You

___

Make love to me

___

Today I Am Not

I Am Not

___

A liar

___

I Am Not

___

A Fake

___

I Am Not

___

An impostor

___

I Am Not

___

A Hypocrite

___

I Am Not

___

A Phony

___

I Am Not

___

A counterfeiter

___

I Am Not

___

A loser

___

I Am Not

___

A misbehaving person

___

I Am Not

___

A trouble maker

___

I Am Not

___

A dismantling person

___

      This day, I am a person of God…

AMEN…

DAY 30
Today I Prophecy This Pray Up-On My Life

I am wearing the coat of victory and I am in the presence of worship. You have stripped me of all impurity and unimpressionable things and words. You have called me from unholy conditions and I am delighted to be around you. You stand in between my sorrow and my joy and hold the hand of both, pain comfort. You stand in between danger and opportunity and you cause them to come together for my good.

When devastation comes you shake your finger in the face of my darkest hour and it moves out of the way of my daylight. The body of Christ is coming towards its greater moment and I remember the path of pain that leads me to the mountain. When I hear you in the wilderness I rush towards your voice. Your Spirit gives life to those that are in the places of death. Your love is unprocessed.

I will parent the ways of love. You are the muse, the scene of your wondrous works. I will priest over the disable and I will go into the place of God for this world. I enter in with truth around my neck and the fragrance of the holy place has consumed my person. Flood me with your words and allow me to feel your voice behind me. I care about the lost. I care about soles and I call in all that will come to the arms of Christ.

I am not exempt from the fight. I am not excused from my crossing. I am free from the rope of religion that tries to lynch itself around the neck of the body. Now is the time for the bleaching of the soul and I give my garment to be washed and brightened, to be white as snow. To Him that sits on the throng and unto the lamb, He shall be blessed.

My mind is in the hands of my maker and it is being reshaped in the wisdom that was known before time. Who can hide from your all seeing eye? Who can lean away from the grasp of your hand, no one. No not one. The parting of the waters is in your mouth and you will drown all of my enemies. The protection of the Father is all around me and the presence of His wings I hear in the distance. I am now in the confidence of my Father.

I prophecy through out the world that the body of Christ move universally by outreaching, pulling into the saving power of God. People everywhere are hungry for God knowingly and unknowingly. I praise God for the body of Christ in the form of her wedding. God is undoubtingly preparing His bride for her wedding. God has always met the needs of His bride. God is inspecting His building for a day of days and I will be ready when He comes for His bride. In the timing of wedding the bride shall come and the beauty of the bride will come covered in the Glory of the Groom.

I Prophecy This Prayer Up-on My Pastor

Day 31 is special because it's rare within the calendar year. Just as this day is rare so is your pastor. You can pray this prophetic prayer each and everyday. Your pastor is in special need of you speaking the blessings of God upon their life. This is an opportunity for you to give back to the ministry of the Lord, which has taken on the mission of covering your life in the Lord.

Why Should I Pray For My Pastor?

Because my pastor needs me
_____

Because I need my pastor
_____

The bible teaches that I should
_____

For my pastor to have great strength
_____

For my pastor to have great boldness in God
_____

For my pastor to have great spiritual insight

Because the gifts of the Spirit need to be in operation within my pastor

---

My pastor needs the ability to do

My pastors family needs my prays and support

My pastor needs to operate and communicate in the Spirit of the LORD

My Pastor needs the love and understanding of the church and surrounding outside areas in order to affect the community as a whole.

MY PASTOR NEEDS MY PRAYERS AND SUPPORT…

God Bless My Pastor. AMEN…

DAY 31

DAY 31
Today I Prophecy This Pray Up-On My Life

<u>My Daily Prayer Confession For My Pastor</u>

We, the people, the body of believers live in perfect harmony and full agreement with the Word of God. There is no division amongst us. Every service is full of Gods' love, His praise, His presence, His revelation, and His power. We are bold in our witness and reigning through the blood of Jesus, over principalities and powers of darkness. We are doers of the Word of God and are experiencing success and victory in every area of our lives. We are redeemed from poverty, sickness and spiritual death, and no weapon formed against us will prosper.

Father God, we thank you that our pastor is filled with the Spirit of wisdom and revelation in the knowledge of you. My pastor is fulfilling your perfect purpose and the plan for pastors' life. Pastor hears the voice of the Good Shepherd and the voice of a stranger my pastor will not follow. We pray that the Spirit of wisdom, knowledge, counsel, might and understanding will guide pastor in every meeting, activity, and conversation that pastor engages in. I thank you that pastor gives continually to prayer, and to the ministry of the Word.

We thank you that pastor studies the Word of

God diligently to feed your flock. I pray that pastors' speech and his preaching are in demonstration of the Spirit and of power. We pray that pastor is skilled in the Word of righteousness and that pastor speaks boldly the prophetic Word of God. Pastor fully preaches the gospel of Christ, rightly dividing the Word of truth, with signs and wonders confirming the Word preached. Pastor is a great person of prayer and a Godly example for all of us.

We thank you, that through the blood of Jesus, pastor is protected from all harm. Pastor is the redeemed of the LORD and is in covenant with You, Jehovah God, therefore sickness and disease, poverty and lack, fear and oppression have no power over my pastor. I praise you Father that my pastor is walking in divine health and pastors' soul prospers because of meditation in your Word day and night.

We thank you that pastor enjoys free time without interruption and is refreshed and rested for every day work, my pastors youth is restored like the eagles. No weapon formed against pastor shall prosper, and every living tongue that is raised against pastor shall be silenced. Thank you Father that your blessing overtakes my pastor, because pastor harkens diligently to your voice.

I cancel every attack of the wicked one against my pastor, to bring deception, distractions, hindrances and temptations into their life. Devil, you are bound in Jesus' name, and have no authority over all pastors and their families, or their possessions. We cover our pastors' family with the blood of Jesus, and at the command of Jesus the releasing of the angels of God ministers over them, and bring them into God's best every day of their lives.

Father, we thank you that you have opened doors of utterance for our pastors' to proclaim boldly the gospel with signs following. My pastor is teaching us how to live independent of this world system and have dominion over it. My pastor has clarity of vision, unhindered by ungodly sources of input. My pastor is always in the right place at the right time, with the right information and the right understanding. My pastor fellowships with leaders of like faith and has set a new standard of excellence for the body of Christ. All hidden things of darkness are revealed to my pastor and are made manifest by the light. We give you praise for the anointing of increase that is upon pastors' life and whatsoever pastor does prospers. We as a body of believers boldly confess the promises in your Word that overtakes our pastors and our churches. Life and death are in the power of my tongue, therefore this day I speak life!

I speak with faith and power that pastor _____ is the God given root for this body of believers.

I speak this prophetically, by the mouth of God, and with power and prayer in the precious name of Jesus, Amen…

Note To The Reader

Just before this manuscript was proofed God gave the revelation and birth place for this term and book title, **"The Prophetic Prayer"**. So, I returned and entered this final section. After I wrote this book God lead me to Hanna's prayer in 1 Samuel chapter 2. Hanna, not only prayed for a son she was also speaking prophetically over the people and purpose of Israel. These first three words have become very meaningful to me, "and Hanna prayed". And this is her prayer and prophecy, ("Prophetic Prayer"). This is "The Prophetic Prayer".

1 Samuel 2:1-21

And Hannah prayed, and said, My heart rejoiceth in the LORD, mine horn is exalted in the LORD: my mouth is enlarged over mine enemies; because I rejoice in thy salvation. [There is] none holy as the LORD: for [there is] none beside thee: neither [is there] any rock like our God. Talk no more so exceeding proudly; let [not] arrogancy come out of your mouth: for the LORD [is] a God of knowledge, and by him actions are weighed. The bows of the mighty men [are] broken, and they that stumbled are girded with strength. [They that were] full have hired out themselves for bread;

and [they that were] hungry ceased: so that the barren hath born seven; and she that hath many children is waxed feeble. The LORD killeth, and maketh alive: he bringeth down to the grave, and bringeth up. The LORD maketh poor, and maketh rich: he bringeth low, and lifteth up. He raiseth up the poor out of the dust, [and] lifteth up the beggar from the dunghill, to set [them] among princes, and to make them inherit the throne of glory: for the pillars of the earth [are] the LORD'S, and he hath set the world upon them. He will keep the feet of his saints, and the wicked shall be silent in darkness; for by strength shall no man prevail. The adversaries of the LORD shall be broken to pieces; out of heaven shall he thunder upon them: the LORD shall judge the ends of the earth; and he shall give strength unto his king, and exalt the horn of his anointed. And Elkanah went to Ramah to his house. And the child did minister unto the LORD before Eli the priest. Now the sons of Eli [were] sons of Belial; they knew not the LORD. And the priests' custom with the people [was, that], when any man offered sacrifice, the priest's servant came, while the flesh was in seething, with a fleshhook of three teeth in his hand; And he struck [it] into the pan, or kettle, or caldron, or pot; all that the fleshhook brought up the priest took for himself. So they did in Shiloh unto all the Israelites that came thither. Also before they burnt the fat, the priest's servant came, and said to the man that sacrificed, Give flesh to roast for the priest; for he will not have sodden flesh of thee, but raw.

And [if] any man said unto him, Let them not fail to burn the fat presently, and [then] take [as much] as thy soul desireth; then he would answer him, [Nay]; but thou shalt give [it me] now: and if not, I will take [it] by force. Wherefore the sin of the young men was very great before the LORD: for men abhorred the offering of the LORD. But Samuel ministered before the LORD, [being] a child, girded with a linen ephod. Moreover his mother made him a little coat, and brought [it] to him from year to year, when she came up with her husband to offer the yearly sacrifice. And Eli blessed Elkanah and his wife, and said, The LORD give thee seed of this woman for the loan which is lent to the LORD. And they went unto their own home. And the LORD visited Hannah, so that she conceived, and bare three sons and two daughters. And the child Samuel grew before the LORD.

The Sinner's Prayer

Dear LORD Jesus. I realize that I am a sinner and I am unworthy of your Holiness. I can not stand in your presence because my flesh is a vessel of filthy sin. But I am asking you to come into my life, clean me up and qualify my person unto righteousness. Reach into my life and change all of my sinful ways into a life of holiness. I am giving you complete authority over my life and my heart is open to you. I believe that you gave your son Jesus to die for the world and that includes me. I believe that you are one God in three persons and I am asking you to come in and save me now. Cover me with the blood of your Son and fill me now with the promise of your Spirit. Now I am yours.
In Jesus name I pray, Amen…

Welcome to the body of Christ.

Pastor Bernard Prince

Reference Page

1. All scripture reference comes from the source of the King James Bible translation.

ISBN # 978-0-692-74484-0
U.S. $14.99 Can. $19.99 or Donation
12gatesministries.org

CPSIA information can be obtained
at www.ICGtesting.com
Printed in the USA
FFOW01n1024101116
29148FF